Container
Water Gardening

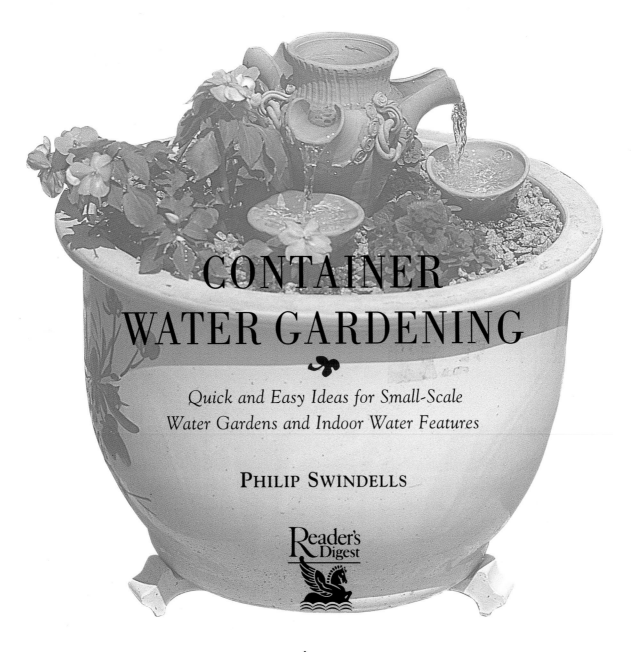

CONTAINER
WATER GARDENING

Quick and Easy Ideas for Small-Scale
Water Gardens and Indoor Water Features

PHILIP SWINDELLS

Reader's Digest

PUBLISHED BY THE READER'S DIGEST ASSOCIATION LIMITED
LONDON

A READER'S DIGEST BOOK

Published by The Reader's Digest Association Limited
11 Westferry Circus
Canary Wharf
London E14 4HE

ISBN 0 276 42399 2

A CIP data record for this book is available from the British Library

This book was designed and produced by
Quarto Publishing plc
The Old Brewery
6 Blundell Street
London N7 9BH

Editor: Ulla Weinberg
Art Editors: Elizabeth Healey, Suzanne Metcalfe-Megginson
Copy Editors: Mary Flower, Gwen Rigby
Designer: Vicki James
Photographers: Ian Howes, Jon Wyand
Illustrators: David Kemp, John Woodcock
Picture Researchers: Gill Metcalfe, Christine Lalla
Art Director: Moira Clinch
Assistant Art Director: Penny Cobb
QUAR.CWG

Manufactured in China by Regent Publishing Services Ltd.
Printed in China by Leefung Asco Printers Ltd.

Contents

OFTEN A WATER FEATURE forms the central focal point in a garden, surrounded by planters spilling over with colourful plants, or perhaps with subtle-coloured foliage in interesting shapes.

Primula beesiana

Introduction

Water is one of the most fascinating elements in the garden. Whether it is a still pond that reflects all around it, or a gentle whispering fountain, it holds a fascination for old and young alike. Water gardening is no longer the prerogative of those with large gardens and generous bank accounts, but a pleasure that can be enjoyed and afforded by all.

The introduction of new materials, such as Low-Density Polyethylene (LDPE) and fibreglass for pool construction, has revolutionised water gardening. Pumps and filters have also become much simpler and smaller over the last few years. Today you don't need large pumps and ugly pump houses to create a beautiful fountain or waterfall. Just place a simple, small, powerful submersible pump in the water and switch it on.

Such innovations mean that smaller units can be successfully created, permitting water features even on the tiniest patio, courtyard or balcony, often planted with miniature aquatics. Water in the garden or outdoor living space is now truly within everyone's range. Container water gardens are not only fashionable but immensely varied and practical, and since they need relatively little maintenance they are ideal for busy people. They also provide an instant effect that in many cases is portable, although, as with other types of gardening, it always takes time for the plants to grow to maturity.

An outdoor container water garden has limited winter appeal. Unlike more extensive garden ponds, which can be arranged to look good even when the plants have died back, container water gardens have insufficient open water surface to make this sort of impact. They are similar to tubs and planters containing flowering plants – a spring and summer-long pleasure, that will often be completely dismantled and stored away during the winter.

The advantage of a container water feature is its versatility. It can be almost anything you want it to be, from a celebration of moving water to a cameo wildlife pool. If the container is carefully chosen, it can become an integral part of the design. The Dutch go in for what they call 'mobile gardens', that is, contained features that can be moved around and changed at will. The plants are grown in inserts, which are lifted and removed from

the larger container as plants pass their best and the display needs changing. They are constantly replaced by new inserts with a fresh specimen of the same plant, or a different one to add interest to the garden feature.

Such configurations of containers, and the ability to change them regularly, make mobile gardens something novel and exciting, especially for gardeners who have inherited stark, barren yards or patios and want a quick way to transform them into attractive garden areas.

Nymphaea 'Aurora'

FISH CAN BE ACCOMMODATED IN MORE SPACIOUS CONTAINERS, but they are generally short-term inhabitants, since few would survive the winter in colder climates in such a small body of water.

A READY-MADE FOUNTAIN KIT provides moving water, and it is one of the few water features that can be used in the shade.

Zantedeschia elliottiana

Container water features can be very diverse, ranging from a miniature waterscape to a geyser gushing through a mound of washed pebbles. If a container can hold water, it is a potential water feature. A wide variety of attractive ready-made water features are available from garden centres, and great sophistication can be achieved with just a screwdriver and the ability to connect a plug to a power supply. If you enjoy DIY, ready-made items may seem less satisfying and the opportunities for creating your own unique feature are legion.

Where space is at a premium and moving water is desired, consider the flexibility offered by a self-contained fountain kit. These are usually wall-mounted with a bowl in a unit that incorporates a small pump, and merely require the addition of water for the desired effect. A whole range of fountains can be used on their own indoors or, with some more elaborate additions, outside. The great advantage of such a modest feature is that it provides moving water for your garden, does not require plants or fish, and is one of the few water features that can be successfully situated in the shade.

There is quite a long history of small water features in the Far East, and oriental gardens are a rich source of inspiration, especially for ideas for fountains. Millstones with water bubbling through them are an adaptation of a traditional oriental idea, and bamboo, currently very fashionable in the West, has long been used by the Japanese in water features. The most popular fountain is the traditional deer scarer, or *shishi-odoshi*, which would make an amusing and decorative focal point for any garden.

Planning and Design

Although container water features are quite small, they still need to be carefully planned if they are to be a practical and visual success. Their position within a garden is also important.

Although the water feature itself may be tastefully planted, it is crucial that, as an element of the garden landscape, it fits into the overall design. This is particularly relevant where the container feature is not easily movable, or is sunk into the ground.

BE SPARING IN YOUR PLANTING Allow the water surface itself to play a part in the water feature.

The first thing to realise is that a container water garden is rarely self-sustaining, and that it is almost impossible to create a natural balance within such a feature. This means that when planting it you have to keep in mind that it will need to be periodically emptied. Therefore, both the position of the feature itself and the planting arrangements must be carefully considered.

Irrespective of the type of water feature, it should be situated in full sun, since most plants require sunlight to thrive. There is little to be gained by positioning water out of the sun – a dancing fountain in the shade does not have much visual impact.

Otherwise, the way in which you introduce water into your garden is very much a matter of personal taste. Small pools and tubs are at their most attractive when

A SELF-CONTAINED water feature with peripheral planting.

viewed at close quarters, so it makes sense to site them close to areas where people sit and relax. Where moving water is involved, especially a fountain, make sure that the site is sheltered. Wind and fitful breezes cause the spray from a fountain to blow around, making it uncomfortable for anyone to sit or garden in the vicinity. It also creates more work, since the reservoir has to be constantly refilled to prevent the pump from running dry and overheating.

A rarely considered advantage of container water gardening is that it provides an opportunity for plant enthusiasts to grow unusual varieties that would not flourish in the rest of the garden. A watertight window box solidly planted with bog garden plants and watered heavily produces a spectacle of fascinating and colourful plants that could otherwise only be enjoyed in a custom-made bog garden.

Most gardeners prefer outdoor features, since they are much easier to control and manage, especially where plants are involved. With indoor features and in warmer climates, tropical plants can be used. Choose varieties that are small and undemanding, as many tropical plants are tall and occupy a lot of space.

When arranging the planting within a container, remember that water is important for its own sake. Do not plant so that the water is entirely lost to view, unless you intend to make a bog garden.

Where plants are meant to be an integral part of a feature, they must be taken into account from the outset. In order to thrive, most of them must be placed in a sunny position. While some of the submerged aquatics can exist with their roots in gravel, all others, except those that float on the surface, must have their roots in aquatic compost. Some will flourish in a modest amount of compost, but you must treat others in the same way you would if you planned to grow them in a

conventional pond: provide them with fair-sized planting containers and adequate amounts of compost.

If you find it difficult to plant up the part of the feature that contains water, consider the possibility of peripheral planting. It is often simpler to create the water part of your design as you want it and then place this in another watertight container in which plants can be grown in an accompanying role. Such plantings often produce a more harmonious, less contrived effect.

While everyone enjoys having fish in a water feature, great caution should be

BRIGHT LIGHT enhances the attraction of water in the garden, especially when the water is moving.

Hosta fortunei 'Gold Standard'

exercised when introducing them into sinks and pots. Fish require a generous water surface to provide them with sufficient oxygen and a reasonable depth of water in order to keep cool. Only large commercial barrels or do-it-yourself constructions are likely to be deep enough and, more importantly, have sufficient water surface area to accomodate fish safely. They

Iris versicolor

can be kept where there is continuous turbulent water, since this provides a ready supply of oxygen, but it is hardly fair to keep them in endless frothing and foaming water.

Unplanted water features, which provide the soothing sound and visual pleasure of water, are often a good idea and are particularly easy to care for, as they require almost no maintenance. Where the water is the main element of the feature and plants do not figure, take into consideration stillness, reflection, movement, colour and sound. Water can bring all these qualities to a garden if you plan the feature thoughtfully. The manner in which you achieve this can be almost as varied as the features themselves, ranging from drips and gushes to trickles and sprays. Moving water can differ widely in its effect, not only with regard to sound but also to light: both overcast skies and contrasting bright sunshine can play an important part. So when planning and designing your water feature, take all of these aspects into account.

Making Made Easy

So many different containers can be used, adapted or created to produce a container water feature that the only limits are your imagination and your creative skills. Where plants and fish are involved, there are a few constraints, but otherwise, provided the construction functions properly, any kind of container will work.

When you have decided on the kind of water feature you want and have considered the questions

IF A CONTAINER WILL HOLD WATER, or it can be made to hold water, it can be turned into a small water feature. The type and arrangement of the plants will determine whether you create a traditional or unusual effect.

of plants and fish, you can turn your attention to cost. Ready-made features can be expensive, but many are excellent value and can be very attractive, particularly when dressed and surrounded by plants of your choice. With small alterations and adaptations many other containers intended for a totally different purpose can be used. For example, you can plug the drainage holes in large ceramic and terracotta pots meant for garden plants with fine aggregate concrete and waterproof them successfully with transparent sealant. Some specialist water gardening centres will do this for you if you don't feel confident doing it yourself. Likewise you can drill pots and rocks to take a small waterfall or fountain outlet; again many aquatics specialists will be happy to do this for you.

While most water features are created in waterproof containers, you should not overlook the possibility of using a pool liner to line any object that is not watertight. There are many different kinds of liner, but the toughest and easiest to mould into a shape without awkward creases are made from LDPE. This can be purchased off the roll and you can buy just as much as you need. Rubber liners, although tough and hard-wearing, are more difficult to install, while polyethylene ones, although much cheaper, have a limited life.

DECORATIVE GARDEN TUBS
offer a low-maintenance water
garden option.

Matteuccia struthiopteris

Making a container water feature can be simple and, for the budget-conscious, economical, since you can use all kinds of ingenious devices. However, the one area where economy should not rule is in purchasing a pump. Go for the best value for money, but be sure that the pump is reliable and will carry out the task that you set it.

Once installed, and providing it is properly constructed, a water feature is one of the easiest and most pleasurable garden features to maintain. I hope the suggestions in this book will inspire and encourage you to create a small oasis in your own garden or courtyard.

Calm Elegance

A pond with still water adds a special quality to gardens and patios of any size. Its surface reflects the movements of the sky and everything around it; and even when confined to a small container, water can bring peace and tranquillity to a garden. Many aquatic plants prefer the conditions in still water, so you can create a lush feature with marginal and bog plants.

Raise the Barrel

You can create a lovely water garden in a barrel or water butt. The barrel must have a consistent water level and not be in use for collecting water – it has to be a feature in its own right.

YOU WILL NEED

- Barrel or water butt
- Stone or hardcore
- Aquatic planting baskets
- Aquatic compost
- Bricks
- Fine gravel

Barrels and water butts may present problems with water levels, as few aquatic plants will tolerate more than 1 m (3 ft) of water. There are two ways to deal with this. The best way is to raise the base level within the barrel with a solid material, which can be stone or anything else that is bulky and will not pollute the water. Top this off with fine gravel to produce a level surface. This provides stability for the barrel and allows you to arrange plants more easily, while from the outside the visual effect is maintained.

If you want to retain the full depth of water in a wooden barrel, you can do this by screwing shelves to the inside, or you can use crosspieces fastened inside the barrel to support the plants. This is also possible with a plastic water butt. The problems of maintaining such a feature are, however, compounded by the fact that the water is so deep and that any debris falling to the bottom can only be removed by dismantling the feature. Whereas if the barrel is only a third full of water, it can be treated in the same way as any other small pond.

The barrel featured here has been planted with a waterlily, *Nymphaea* 'Aurora', as a centrepiece and *Iris laevigata* 'Rose Queen' and *Veronica beccabunga* to dress the edges. The waterlily is grown in a container filled with aquatic compost in the deeper part of the barrel so that it is covered by no more than 50 cm (20 in) of water. Grow the marginal plants in aquatic compost in baskets raised on bricks so that they are just beneath the water. Parrot feather and hornwort, *Myriophyllum aquaticum* and *Ceratophyllum demersum*, provide submerged aquatic plant growth.

PLANTING

1. *Ceratophyllum demersum* (submerged)
2. *Veronica beccabunga*
3. *Myriophyllum aquaticum* (submerged)
4. *Iris laevigata* 'Rose Queen'
5. *Nymphaea* 'Aurora'
6. *Lysimachia nummularia* 'Aurea'

Lowering the Level

Constructed of natural material, a sunken barrel pond fits easily into a more rustic garden setting, becoming part of the localised landscape rather than appearing imposed upon it.

YOU WILL NEED

- Half-barrel
- Pool liner or transparent sealant
- Wood preservative
- Aquatic planting baskets
- Aquatic compost
- Discarded tights
- Bricks or stones

PLANTING

1. *Iris laevigata*
2. *Nymphaea tetragona* 'Helvola'
3. *Typha minima*
4. *Mimulus x hybridus* 'Calypso'

A sunken barrel pond is especially suitable for a colder climate. The earth acts as insulation and the water is less likely to freeze. In most circumstances, hardy aquatic plants, and even small common goldfish, will overwinter without difficulty in such a feature.

Most sunken barrels are made of wood with metal straps, although there are also some very convincing solid plastic kinds available. Wooden barrel pools are generally made from half a barrel of the type that contained a liquid, often whisky or beer. There are some cheaper ones about which have been used for tar or oil products, but these should be avoided. It is best to purchase a new barrel from a garden centre and either seal it with transparent sealant inside, or line it with a plastic pool liner.

When preparing to sink the barrel into the ground, dig the hole to a depth that allows about 10 cm (4 in) of the barrel to protrude above soil level. The effect is much better when the edge is exposed, and the raised edge also prevents inquisitive small animals from falling into the pond. While most barrels sold in garden centres are sufficiently well preserved for general garden use, sinking them into the ground does hasten their demise. So it is advisable to paint preservative on the outside or to tack pool liner to the sides to keep the wood dry. Make sure the liner is a good fit, as any water trapped between it and the barrel can cause rotting.

Planting the barrel is simple. If you want a single waterlily, choose one such as *Nymphaea tetragona* 'Helvola' and grow it in a small planting basket. Although marginal plants such as *Typha minima* and *Iris laevigata* can be planted on the floor of the barrel directly into aquatic compost, there will be no control over their growth or the depth of water over their crowns. They are better grown in aquatic compost in small bags made from old tights and raised to the desired level on bricks or stones set close to the side of the barrel. Add *Mimulus x hybridus* 'Calypso', or alternatively *M. ringens*, for a dash of colour outside the barrel.

In the Sink

❧

Old sinks make wonderful water features. Although the whiteness of the traditional kitchen sink is often disguised, it can provide a happy contrast to a tasteful planting scheme.

YOU WILL NEED

- Old ceramic sink
- Cement and sand mix or plug
- Sealant
- Rocks
- Stones or bricks
- Aquatic planting baskets and latticework pot cover
- Aquatic compost and sand

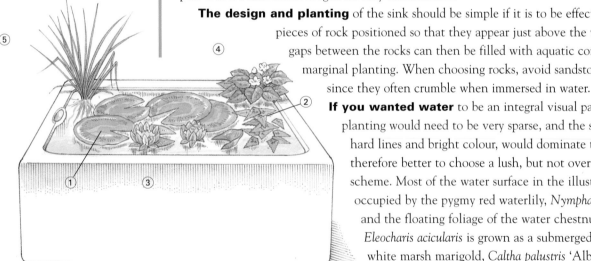

PLANTING

① *Nymphaea tetragona* 'Rubra'

② *Trapa natans*

③ *Eleocharis acicularis* (submerged)

④ *Caltha palustris* 'Alba'

⑤ *Typha minima*

The sink should be positioned in a part of the garden where other plantings can provide a fresh green background. Standing alone on a terrace or patio, it can look a little stark.

Seal the drainage hole, either by inserting a plug or by blocking it up with a fine concrete mix and then painting on a sealant. For the best effect raise the sink on stones or bricks. Not only does this allow for easier drainage from the plug hole, but it also shows off the feature better and puts it at a comfortable height for easy maintenance.

The design and planting of the sink should be simple if it is to be effective. One or two pieces of rock positioned so that they appear just above the water are ideal. The gaps between the rocks can then be filled with aquatic compost to allow for marginal planting. When choosing rocks, avoid sandstone or limestone, since they often crumble when immersed in water.

If you wanted water to be an integral visual part of this design, planting would need to be very sparse, and the sink itself, with its hard lines and bright colour, would dominate the feature. It is therefore better to choose a lush, but not overcrowded, planting scheme. Most of the water surface in the illustrated example is occupied by the pygmy red waterlily, *Nymphaea tetragona* 'Rubra', and the floating foliage of the water chestnut, *Trapa natans*. *Eleocharis acicularis* is grown as a submerged plant and the white marsh marigold, *Caltha palustris* 'Alba', and *Typha minima* as marginal plants.

The eleocharis should be encouraged to carpet the floor of the sink with its fine grassy foliage. To ensure this, place a thin layer of four parts aquatic compost mixed with one part sand on the bottom and plant small groups of the plant into it. Grow the waterlily in a very small basket, such as a latticework pot cover, placed in the centre of the sink. *Caltha* and *Typha* should be planted into aquatic planting baskets and positioned near the edge of the sink. Allow the water chestnut to float about freely.

Eastern Tranquillity

❧

This water feature takes its character from the Orient. It can stand on its own, or be a focal point in a more extensive oriental setting. The planting is representative of the Japanese style.

YOU WILL NEED
- Rectangular bamboo container
- Pool liner
- Square plastic container
- Aquatic planting baskets
- Lime-free compost
- Aquatic compost
- Rocks
- Stones or bricks

PLANTING
① *Iris ensata* 'Queen of the Blues'
② Moss
③ *Typha minima*

Bamboo containers of this type are widely sold as planters for indoor plants or summer annuals on the patio or terrace. Some have plastic or metal inserts to protect the wooden interior. While this is satisfactory for ordinary garden or indoor plants, it is not a reliable protection in a water feature, and you will have to fasten pool liner inside the container to make it watertight. Be sure that any bamboo container you buy has some timber or plywood inside, as it is it is extremely difficult to secure a pool liner to bamboo.

Within the lined planter, place a large plastic pot, preferably a square one without drainage holes, so that you can isolate an area free from water to represent land. Pack compost in and around this pot to keep it in place. Aquatic compost is not necessary, but since the acid-loving *Iris ensata* 'Queen of the Blues' is the main focal plant you should use a lime-free compost. The dwarf Japanese reedmace, *Typha minima*, is grown in a small, open planting basket, placed in the water and raised on a brick or stone if necessary to bring it to within about 5 cm (2 in) of the water surface. This plant should be grown in aquatic compost.

Level off the compost in the container representing the land, and carefully place two rocks on top of it to create a miniature landscape. Avoid rocks that contain calcium, such as limestone; instead choose hard rocks, ideally granite or slate. If they have been well weathered, all the better.

If the feature is to stand in a cool, damp and partially shaded position, the natural look can be enhanced by introducing moss into it. Take pieces of suitable moss with a thin layer of soil and set them as close together as possible on the surface of the compost between the rocks. They should then quickly unite.

Matching Set

❧

This project provides an opportunity to mix and match a water feature to suit your circumstances. It can be moved around the patio or garden like furniture, similar to a Dutch 'mobile garden'.

YOU WILL NEED

The following cut from 12.5 mm (½ in) exterior plywood:
- 2 90 cm x 40 cm (36 in x 16 in); 2 57.5 cm x 40 cm (23 in x 16 in); 1 90 cm x 60 cm (35 in x 24 in)
- 2 60 cm x 35 cm (24 in x 14 in); 2 42.5 cm x 35 cm (17 in x 14 in); 1 60 cm x 45 cm (24 in x 18 in)
- 2 45 cm x 30 cm (18 in x 12 in); 2 30 cm x 27.5 cm (12 in x 11 in); 1 45 cm x 30 cm (18 in x 12 in)

You will also need:
- 18–20 thin round fence posts, split in half
- 48 plastic corner joints
- 12.5 mm (½ in) screws
- 12.5 cm (5 in) nails
- Panel pins
- Wood preservative
- Pool liner
- Hammer, staple gun, saw, screwdriver, drill
- Bricks or inverted planting baskets
- Aquatic planting baskets
- Aquatic compost
- Fine gravel

The interior dimensions of the three containers are: 90 cm x 60 cm x 40 cm (36 in x 24 in x 16 in); 60 cm x 45 cm x 35 cm (24 in x 18 in x 14 in); 45 cm x 30 cm x 30 cm (18 in x 12 in x 12 in).

◁ **ONE**

Place the base board on a flat surface and, making sure the box is square, tack the sides together with panel pins.

▽ **TWO**

Secure the top corners of the box with eight plastic corner joints. This will give the box rigidity.

△ **THREE**

Drop the base into the box and turn the frame upside down.

▽ **FOUR**

Secure the base with eight more corner joints on the outside, positioned about 7.5 cm (3 in) from each corner. These provide support and keep the base off the ground and therefore free from damp. Paint all the surfaces with wood preservative.

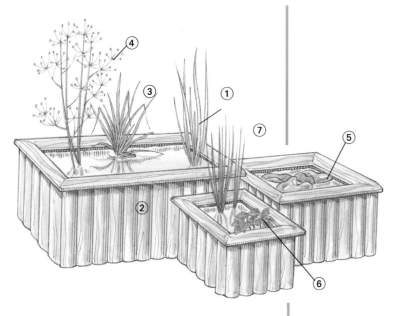

FIVE ▷

Saw the fence posts to length. Since fence posts vary in thickness try them against the box before screwing them in position.

SIX ▷

Overlap the lengths of fence post at the corners to ensure that they fit snugly.

PLANTING

This group of containers offers many opportunities for planting a wide range of aquatics, provided that the water remains still.

① *Acorus calamus* 'Variegatus'
② *Myriophyllum aquaticum* (submerged)
③ *Carex elata* 'Bowles' Golden'
④ *Alisma plantago-aquatica*
⑤ *Nymphaea* 'Aurora'
⑥ *Houttuynia cordata* 'Chameleon'
⑦ *Typha minima*

◁ **SEVEN**

From the remaining fence posts, cut capping logs to size, with their corners cut to 45-degree-angle mitres. Paint the capping logs and fence posts with wood preservative.

Calm Elegance **26**

△ EIGHT

Install the liner and fasten it at the top with staples before fixing the capping. To avoid splitting the capping, drill pilot holes through the wood and hammer in the nails at an angle, pointing towards the middle. This will lock the top in place.

▽ TEN

Plant the aquatics in planting baskets filled with aquatic compost. Top-dress the baskets with a generous layer of fine gravel to prevent the compost from clouding the water.

△ ELEVEN

Plant the waterlily *Nymphaea* 'Aurora' in a planting basket and place it in position.

△ NINE

The containers are ready for planting. In order to bring the plants to the correct level, raise them on inverted planting baskets or bricks.

TWELVE ▷

Soak the freshly planted aquatics with water before adding the main body of water to the containers. This forces out the air and prevents the compost from escaping into the water.

Purely Plants

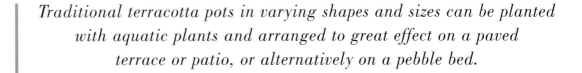

Traditional terracotta pots in varying shapes and sizes can be planted with aquatic plants and arranged to great effect on a paved terrace or patio, or alternatively on a pebble bed.

YOU WILL NEED

- Three light-coloured terracotta pots in different sizes and shapes
- Aquatic compost
- Fine gravel

PLANTING

1. *Butomus umbellatus*
2. *Iris laevigata* 'Rose Queen'
3. *Juncus effusus* 'Spiralis'
4. *Lysimachia nummularia*
5. *Lysimachia nummularia* 'Aurea'
6. *Pontederia cordata*
7. *Sagittaria sagittifolia* 'Flore Pleno'
8. *Iris laevigata* 'Variegata'
9. *Iris laevigata* 'Colchesteri'

Where you position the containers depends on the effect you seek, whether one of focus and contrast, or soft harmony. On a hard, reflective surface such as glazed tiles, the design and look of the pots are very important, but less so when the pots are partially hidden by other plantings.

Most terracotta pots are suitable for this kind of water feature. Because the volume of water they contain is relatively small, it will freeze quickly, and you will need to bring them indoors during the winter in colder areas. It is quite possible, therefore, to use some fine, fancy pots that are not frost resistant. In winter, drain off the water, but leave the plants growing in the pots and place them in a frost-free, but cool, place. They will come to no harm and can be started into growth again next spring.

For the best effect, in summer you should treat the pots as if they were miniature swamps. Fill the containers at least two-thirds full with aquatic compost, plant them up, top them off with fine gravel, and then add water. Plants should only rarely stand in more than 15 cm (6 in) of water. There is a potential problem with mosquitoes with this type of feature, since the water is deep enough for their larvae to survive and yet not deep enough to house fish to eat them. You can solve this problem by adding a drop of cooking oil to the water every couple of weeks; it creates a film over the water surface that is harmless to plants but prevents mosquito larvae coming up for air. In this feature, the appearance of the water surface is not important, since it is rarely visible as the pots become completely filled with plants.

In your planting arrangments, avoid vigorous, tall plants, which may unbalance the container both visually and literally. Use creeping plants such as the golden-leafed *Lysimachia nummularia* 'Aurea' to provide tumbling foliage over the edge. Other marginal plants in this feature include *Butomus umbellatus*, varieties of *Iris laevigata*, *Pontederia cordata* and *Juncus effusus* 'Spiralis', but use no more than two or three of the more upright types for each container if the plants are all to live happily together.

On the Shelf

❧

A delightful miniature water garden can be created in a window box. For the best effect, think carefully about its position and planting scheme.

YOU WILL NEED

- Plastic trough or window box insert
- Aquatic compost
- Latticework plant pot holders or covers

PLANTING

① *Lysimachia nummularia* 'Aurea'

② *Mimulus x hybridus* 'Calypso'

③ *Mimulus x hybridus* 'Queen's Prize'

④ *Primula vialii*

⑤ *Sisyrinchium angustifolium*

A successful water feature can be created in a window box, but remember that the weight of saturated compost and water is considerable and that the window box cannot be situated in the conventional position with the usual brackets. If you want it next to the window, it must be positioned on a solid window ledge.

While this water feature does not necessarily have standing water in it, the soil must be saturated, and so a watertight container is essential. There are many troughs and window box inserts to choose from. Generally troughs have no drainage holes and are perfect for the job; the inserts that fit into traditional window boxes mostly have drainage holes which will have to be blocked and made reliably watertight.

Bog garden plants are the best choice for this kind of situation. They can either be planted directly into the compost in the trough or box, or placed side by side in small planting containers. Plant-pot holders or covers serve this purpose well, since they have open sides and come in sizes that fit readily into a window box. Most proper aquatic planting baskets are too large. Although a solidly planted feature may look slightly more natural, plants growing side by side in pots are isolated from one another and are easier to control, since their roots will not grow together. They can also be easily lifted out for division or replacement.

Select fibrous-rooted plants rather than those that produce creeping underground stems or rhizomes; they are much better behaved and reduce the need for control to a mimimum. Mimulus and primulas are excellent for such features. *Mimulus x hybridus* 'Calypso' and M. x *hybridus* 'Queen's Prize' provide summer-long colour and *Sisyrinchium angustifolium* gives a variation in stature and habit. *Primula vialii* produces startling lilac and red flowers in late spring before the mimulus start blooming. Although mimulus and primulas are perennials, in a window box they are best treated as annuals and replaced regularly, thereby ensuring a fresh, colourful and long-lasting display.

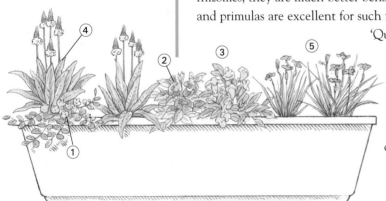

Watering

The opportunities for creating interesting small water features are enormous. Here, a good-looking metal watering can is used as the starting point for an attractive feature.

Any container that holds water can be used to make a water feature. One of the most common objects in the garden is the watering can, which, when planted up, can be a very attractive water garden feature.

By situating it on a paved or gravel base, as if it were simply standing out in the garden, but in a position where it is a focal point and surrounded by mixed planting, it will appear a natural part of the garden scene, just as planted wheelbarrows do. For the small garden or yard with limited space a single watering can is sufficient, but where there is a little more room, two cans of different shapes and sizes can be used together to complement one another.

It is possible to use a watering can as the outlet for a pump, the water filling the can and spraying from the spout. However, quite a powerful pump is required to lift the water sufficiently to make the water spray rather than dribble. It can be done, but it is more successful as a feature within a larger pool setting.

A wide range of plants will adapt to the growing conditions in a watering can, which can be equated with those of the pool margin or bog garden, depending upon how much water is added. Visually, a long, low can works best with frothing, tumbling plants such as *Veronica beccabunga* and *Lysimachia nummularia* 'Aurea' growing out of the top and spilling over. An upright can will take taller subjects better. Choose an elegant plant, such as the rushlike pink-flowered *Butomus umbellatus*, as a focal point.

Use aquatic compost as the growing medium and fill the watering can halfway. Do not plant anything in the can until the foliage is tall enough to come above the rim. The emerging plants will be weak if you plant them initially in the gloom of the watering can's interior, and they will not grow well when they finally emerge.

PLANTING
1. *Butomus umbellatus*
2. *Lysimachia nummularia* 'Aurea'
3. *Veronica beccabunga*

Mosaic Sink Garden

❧

A water garden in a sink is ideal for a small garden or patio. It looks great placed beside a rock garden planted with tiny alpines, since the most suitable plants for it are also miniature.

YOU WILL NEED

This project utilises an old sink, but it can be adapted to similar troughs and containers. Before starting work on the decoration, block up the plug hole. The hole is not likely to be of a conventional size in an old sink, but if you are lucky you may find a suitable plug. If you do, raise the sink slightly from the ground, perhaps on four bricks and when it requires emptying, remove the plug and simply let the water run away. Where a suitable plug cannot be found, block up the hole with a mixture of coarse sand and cement and paint over it with a sealant.

- Old sink
- Odd tiles and tile off-cuts available from DIY stores
- Tile cutter
- Tile adhesive and grout
- Fine gravel
- Aquatic planting baskets
- Aquatic compost

◁ **ONE**
Cut the tiles into small squares of varying sizes and sort them into colour batches.

▽ **TWO**
Before you stick the tile pieces to the sink, lay out the mosaic design on a piece of cardboard.

△ **THREE**
Positioning the tile pieces is a slow process, so apply a generous amount of tile adhesive over only a small area at a time.

△ **FOUR**
Build up the pattern steadily, attaching the tiles with a slight twisting movement in order to bed them down firmly.

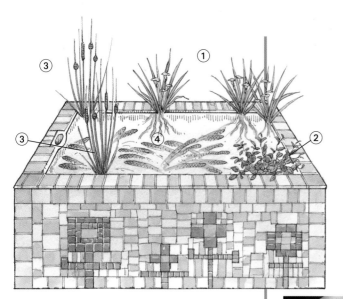

FIVE ▷

When the design on one side is complete, wipe away the excess tile adhesive with a cloth. Allow the mosaic to dry before continuing with another side.

PLANTING

It is easy to overplant a sink, so use a minimal number of plants of the restrained varieties. Even so, they will require regular cutting back during the summer months to keep them compact. There are many plants that can be grown in a sink, but these are the ones used in this feature.

① *Sisyrinchium californicum* var. *brachypus*
② *Mimulus* x *hybridus* 'Calypso'
③ *Typha minima*
④ *Lagarosiphon major* (submerged)

◁ **SIX**

When the sides are completed, cap the edge with slightly larger tile pieces. Make sure they are flush with the outside edge.

SEVEN ▷

To fill in the gaps between the tiles, finish with a coating of grout, wiping it off quickly and smoothly with a damp cloth.

▽ EIGHT

Allow the sink to dry completely before moving it into position or planting it.

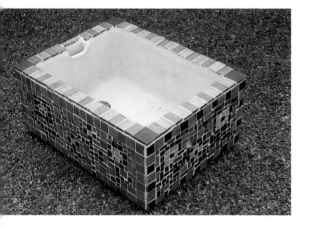

▽ NINE

It is preferable to grow all the plants in separate baskets or they will become invasive and unmanageable. Spread gravel on the bottom to disguise the white finish and mound it in the corners to form planting platforms. Put the plants in position, adjusting the depth of water over them by redistributing the gravel beneath the planting baskets.

△ TEN

Run water gently into the sink over a piece of plastic in order not to disturb the gravel.

△ ELEVEN

Position the submerged plant in the water. The initial cloudiness of the water is caused largely by the gravel, but the sediment will soon settle and the water will become clear.

Magic in Movement

Bring your patio or garden to life with the sound and colour of moving water. Whether it is a gentle trickle, a gushing spray or a bubbling spout, few other elements can change the mood in a garden or patio as radically as moving water sparkling in bright sunshine. Small submersible pumps make it easy to install these features.

Linked with Water

❧

This barrel garden comprises two half-barrel tubs of different sizes positioned so that they create a rustic, flowing water feature. The turbulent water still allows for a number of planting options.

YOU WILL NEED

- Two half-barrels of different sizes, linked by an ornamental pump (prefabricated)
- Submersible pump
- Aquatic planting baskets
- Aquatic compost

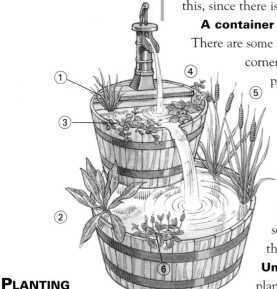

PLANTING

① *Acorus calamus* 'Variegatus'
② *Alisma plantago-aquatica*
③ *Caltha palustris*
④ *Lysimachia nummularia* 'Aurea'
⑤ *Typha latifolia*
⑥ *Veronica beccabunga*

The water in this feature is circulated from the lower barrel into the ornamental pump from which it cascades down into the two barrels. The pump is partially encased in the barrels, which gives a pleasing unity to the feature. A strong submerged pump is required when creating a feature like this, since there is a considerable lift and substantial water flow.

A container water garden of this kind should be positioned in an open, sunny position. There are some advantages to positioning the decorative pump with its back to a wall, or in a corner, although it might look a little stark. Alternatively, a position in a more heavily planted area of the garden would be suitable because of the pump's rustic, 'old world' appearance.

Plants can be grown in the barrels, despite the turbulent water, provided that suitable varieties are selected. The vigorous-growing reedmace, *Typha latifolia*, fits in well here, although it can rarely be grown elsewhere in a container water garden. The area at the back of the lower barrel, where the upper one overlaps it, is an ideal spot as it is sufficiently sheltered for the typha. Its planting basket, filled with aquatic compost, can be successfully secured to the barrel so that it does not topple over into the water. In addition, the height of the typha will help to link the two barrels visually.

Unlike some other small, planted water features, here you can establish creeping plants in the same container as tall marginals such as the typha. *Lysimachia nummularia* 'Aurea', for example, will thrive much better when planted into the bottom of the barrel and allowed to tumble over the edge, rather than being established in individual planting baskets that would also take up limited water space. Link such a planting with other vigorous marginal plants, such as the water plantain, *Alisma plantago-aquatica*. This attractive feature also includes the variegated sweet flag, *Acorus calamus* 'Variegatus', the marsh marigold *Caltha palustris* and cheerful tumbling *Veronica beccabunga* to extend the season of interest.

Pot Up a Fountain

Plants are not always necessary in a container water feature. Water trickling gently over stones is evocative of a mountain stream, an effect that can easily be achieved in a small decorative container.

YOU WILL NEED

- Small decorative container
- Plastic bowl or pot with holes
- Submersible pump
- Drilled focal stone
- Pebbles

Many aquatic plants dislike moving water and cannot be used in water gardens with a fountain jet. In this feature, the water itself is the focal point. The container need not be enormous, but it should be able to accommodate a submersible pump in a small chamber with rocks or stones covering the top. An inverted plastic bowl or pot that almost fills the container and comes to within 5–10 cm (2–4 in) of the top is ideal. This should have holes in it to permit the water free passage. Essentially, the decorative pot or bowl is full of water, with the stones or pebbles disguising the chamber from view. The maximum volume of water is essential.

The focal stone in the container should have a hole drilled through it, into which you push the pump outlet. Sandstone or limestone are the easiest to drill, although it is possible to buy ready-drilled stones at specialist aquatic centres. Make sure that the stone is not freshly quarried, but has a hardened, weathered finish, otherwise it will erode and gritty material will settle in the container and may block the pump.

It is important to check a pebble fountain constantly for water loss. The endless exposure of the water to air and warmth causes a surprising amount of evaporation, and 10–15 cm (4–6 in) of water can be lost in a couple of days. Ideally, the water level should be just above the top of the chamber. The only problem that this can cause is a deposit of algae, rather like a tidemark, along the edge of the stones. To prevent this occurring, and to ensure that the water remains clear and the pebbles fresh and shiny, regularly add an algicide to the water. This will ensure that the water remains crystal clear and sparkles in the sunshine.

Going *Shishi-Odoshi*

A shishi-odoshi is a traditional Japanese water feature made from bamboo and operated by moving water. The loud cracking sound that the hollow tube gives was originally intended to scare away deer.

There are several configurations for this water feature, but the most usual consists of two upright bamboo supports holding a more slender rocking tube. Water from a chamber below is pumped up through one of the hollow upright canes and, by means of a small bamboo spout near the top, pours into the waiting rocking tube. The weight overbalances the tube forward and the water pours out. In doing this, it knocks against either a strategically positioned short length of bamboo towards the top of the supports or, as shown here, a stone placed at the bottom.

A chamber sunk into the ground is necessary to operate a *shishi-odoshi*. It should contain a submersible pump that has sufficient power to raise the water without straining. Provided that the pump is completely covered by water, you can use a wide, shallow container. One advantage of this is that it reduces the required lift of the pump; it also means that you can accommodate plants that enjoy really wet conditions.

Once the container and pump are installed, position the *shishi-odoshi* close to the side of the sunken container, with the spout pointing towards the middle of it. It is easier to ensure that the upright supports are secure if they are in the ground than if they are fastened to the container. The container must be covered with material such as fine wire-mesh reinforcing, which can support the weight of pebbles or cobbles and is porous at the same time. By enlarging parts of the mesh, you can make provision for plants to grow through.

There is a wide choice of plants for such a feature, but for the most satisfactory appearance you should choose Japanese plants and those that look oriental. Use bog garden plants that can stand in water with their crowns just above the surface, or arrange some of the planting in the areas near the edge of the feature. *Iris laevigata* 'Colchesteri' can stand very happily in water, but hostas such as 'Thomas Hogg', *Primula beesiana* and *P. bulleyana*, as well as bog garden ferns such as *Onoclea sensibilis*, are happier in the slightly drier conditions around the edge.

Down by the Old Millstone

A millstone with water bubbling through the centre is a pleasing way to enjoy the sound and appearance of water with the benefit of easy maintenance and, if children are around, perfect safety.

YOU WILL NEED

- Fibreglass or reconstituted stone millstone
- Large container
- Submersible pump
- String
- Large-gauge and fine wire-mesh reinforcing, or reinforcing rods
- Large pebbles or cobbles
- Aquatic planting baskets
- Aquatic compost

PLANTING

① *Butomus umbellatus*
② *Lysimachia nummularia* 'Aurea'
③ *Veronica beccabunga*

Millstone fountains have become a part of many modern gardens. Genuine millstones are few and far between, but in recent years both manufacturers of reconstituted stone and moulders of fibreglass have begun to create very convincing substitutes. Fibreglass millstones are easily manoeuvrable, lightweight features.

When preparing to install a millstone water feature choose a shallow container that is at least 15 cm (6 in) larger all round than the millstone. This way you can arrange pebbles or cobbles decoratively around the edge where the overflowing water seeps through, leaving one or two places where plants can be introduced.

Sink the container into the ground and install a submersible pump. Attach a piece of string to the outlet tube so that it can be pulled through the centre of the millstone when required. You must provide a secure base for the millstone to rest on; this can be made from either wire-mesh reinforcing or metal reinforcing rods. A large-gauge wire mesh is required for the main support, and you will need finer wire mesh to lay over the top to prevent pebbles from dropping through the gaps. Once the support system is in place, position the millstone carefully, then draw the string fastened to the outlet through the centre of the stone and attach a simple jet to it. Set pebbles or cobbles around the millstone to disguise the pump chamber completely.

Since the millstone is such a strong feature on its own, any associated planting must be carefully arranged. Use more discreet plants such as *Veronica beccabunga* and *Lysimachia nummularia* 'Aurea' around the edge to soften the appearance of the pebbles, and slender plants such as *Butomus umbellatus* to provide height. You can establish these plants in low, flat baskets and place them on top of the reinforced support, surrounding and covering them with pebbles. Alternatively, you can position them within the chamber and raise their baskets on bricks. However, this reduces the water volume and means that the plants have to emerge between the reinforcing, which is not always satisfactory. You will find it much easier to control the plants if you plant them among the pebbles.

Pocketing the Best

❧

A traditional strawberry pot can be turned into an attractive water feature if lined with a piece of pool liner or a waterproof pot insert. Plant the outside pockets with luscious trailing plants.

YOU WILL NEED

- Strawberry pot
- Miniature submersible pump
- Pool liner or plastic insert
- Adhesive
- General-purpose compost

PLANTING

① *Lobelia erinus* 'Blue Trailing'

Ideally, you should use a plastic pot insert for this feature since it has the necessary rigidity. If you cannot find a suitable-sized insert, a piece of pool liner will do the job. Make sure that it is kept firmly in place by sticking the liner to the inside of the strawberry pot with dabs of adhesive, and neatly finish off the edge.

Water is circulated by a miniature submersible pump that weighs about 500 g (1 lb) and nestles neatly in the bottom of the pot. Carefully slip the cable down between the insert and the inner wall of the pot and thread it through one of the lower planting holes that will be turned away from the main line of view.

The pockets in the pot should be filled with general-purpose compost. Unlike a conventionally planted strawberry pot, it is not possible to work both inside and outside the pot and you will have to insert the compost and each plant from the outside. As relatively little compost is available for each plant, you will have to select suitable plant types and water them regularly.

The trailing *Lobelia erinus* is one of the most suitable plants for this kind of feature. It tolerates having only a little soil for its roots and produces good-quality foliage and masses of blue flowers throughout most of the summer. To ensure that it continues to flower well once the small amount of compost has become exhausted, apply a foliar feed regularly. Any liquid feed applied to the sparse amount of soil in the pockets is likely to be wasted, since most of it will simply run down the outside of the pot; fertiliser tablets are a better option.

You can also try using trailing plants that are grown for their attractive tumbling foliage rather than their flowers, especially the golden-leafed *Lysimachia nummularia* 'Aurea' and its green-leafed, yellow-flowered parent *L. nummularia*.

Be Classical!

Fountain masks offer great opportunities for introducing moving water into a limited space, especially where the area is surrounded by a wall, fence or trellis.

YOU WILL NEED

- Lion's head wall mask
- Submersible pump
- Plastic bucket
- Paving slabs
- Ball valve (optional)
- Large pebbles or cobbles
- Fine gravel
- Aquatic planting baskets
- Aquatic compost

PLANTING

① *Mimulus luteus*

② *Pontederia cordata*

③ *Potamogeton crispus*
    (submerged)

The fountain mask is simple to install, and it is easy to ensure that it functions properly. You could introduce a submersible pump into the small pool into which the mask spouts, but it is difficult to disguise the pump and the outflow up to the mask. It is far better when installing this type of feature to construct a lower chamber, or sump, to accommodate the pump safely – a standard plastic bucket is ideal.

Sink the bucket into the ground and place the pool for the fountain on paving slabs laid over the top of the bucket. Arrange these carefully so that you are able to gain access to the pump when necessary. Often the pool will be provided with an overflow, rather like that on a kitchen sink, which links into the sump below via a tube or pipe; if it does not have a built-in overflow, you will need to construct one. The pump circulates the water up into the mask, from where it drops down into the pool and then overflows back into the sump. The water level in the sump will require regular topping up, which you can do simply by running a hose into the pool periodically. It is also quite easy to construct a ball valve arrangement in the sump itself, which will ensure that it is topped up automatically.

Arranging the outlet so that it is not seen can take some ingenuity. On a fence or trellis it is fairly simple: fasten the mask to an upright to secure it, and hide the outlet behind the same upright. Where the mask is fastened to a wall it is a little more difficult. With a plasterboard wall a hole must be drilled through it so that the outlet pipe can be passed up out of sight behind it; solid walls can usually accommodate the pipe in the central cavity.

Aquatics with floating leaves and true floating plants dislike the conditions in a fountain pool with constantly running water. It is much better to use marginal plants, such as the yellow musk, *Mimulus luteus* and the pickerel, *Pontederia cordata*, together with a submerged aquatic, such as *Potamogeton crispus*, which is tolerant of disturbed water. Put large pebbles or cobbles into the pool to provide some height, and add some fine gravel. Plant the aquatic plants into separate baskets filled with aquatic compost and position them around the edge of the pool. The *Potamogeton* is planted straight into the gravel.

Pouring Water

The tilted urn appears as if it has been left lying on its side and the water it contains is spilling out. It is actually seated on pebbles in a container, with a pump situated beneath to circulate the water.

YOU WILL NEED

- Ceramic or terracotta urn and container, both with a hole in the bottom
- Plastic or polypropylene container
- Submersible pump
- Large-gauge wire-mesh reinforcing
- Weed-suppressing fabric
- Large pebbles or cobbles
- Aquatic planting baskets

PLANTING

1. *Caltha palustris* 'Flore Pleno'
2. *Iris laevigata* 'Variegata'
3. *Lobelia* x *speciosa* 'Queen Victoria'
4. *Mimulus* x *hybridus* 'Malibu'

In this feature, the urn sits on a base of pebbles within a terracotta or ceramic container. The water is circulated via a pump and spills from the urn's rim back onto the pebbles, so the whole construction – urn, container and pump – has to be seated within another, larger base container to avoid loss of water.

Any container can be used as a base, either raised or sunken. Its main function is to serve as the chamber from which water is circulated by a submerged pump, but here it is also used to establish complementary marginal or bog plants.

If the base container is to be sunk into the ground, as here, it need only be made of strong plastic or polypropylene and will, therefore, be light and easy to install. Position the pump on the bottom of the base container and disguise the cable with cobbles, pebbles or plants where it emerges. Install the plants in their planting baskets and raise them on bricks on the floor of the base container. Place large-gauge wire-mesh reinforcing over the top so that it covers the entire surface of the base container, with the plants just poking through. Put a layer of weed-suppressing fabric over the top, with holes cut in it where the plants emerge and some small slits made in other areas to allow the water to filter through to the container beneath. Then cover the area with pebbles. Position the terracotta container on top of this, feed the pump connection through the hole in its base, and fill it with pebbles. Place the urn on top of the pebbles and feed the pump connection through the hole in its lower end. The water can now be circulated back into the base container.

Although an attractive feature on its own, it looks much better when dressed with plants of varying growth habits. Use the double-flowered marsh marigold, *Caltha palustris* 'Flore Pleno', for an early spring show. Follow this with the blue-flowered *Iris laevigata* 'Variegata' with its handsome swordlike leaves, which form a striking contrast to the red-purple foliage of *Lobelia* x *speciosa* 'Queen Victoria'. The easygoing, summer-long flowering *Mimulus* x *hybridus* 'Malibu' is an attractive addition. Alternative plants for this feature could be *Caltha palustris* 'Alba' or *Typha minima*, with its grassy foliage and small, brown, poker-shaped heads.

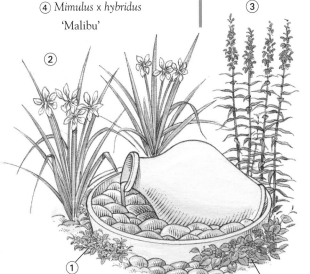

Trickling Trio

A pebbled area with strategically placed bubbling pots and occasional planting to soften the harshness of the stones makes this one of the most visually appealing water features.

YOU WILL NEED

- Three ceramic or terracotta pots
- Large submersible pump
- Large container or tank
- Large-gauge wire-mesh reinforcing
- Epoxy glue
- Large pebbles or cobbles
- Aquatic planting baskets
- Aquatic compost

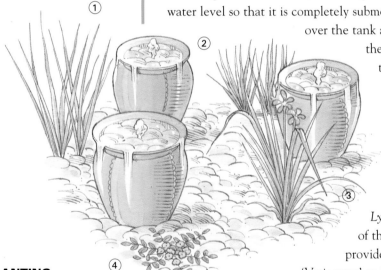

For this project, you can use small pumps in each of the three pots, each contained in a chamber. In order to hide the pump cables, you need to thread them through holes in the bottom of the pots – either ready-made drainage holes, or holes you have drilled yourself – and seal in the cables with epoxy glue.

If you prefer, a stronger, single pump can be installed in a sunken chamber, as here, with three outlets, one to each of the pots. You will need to sink a large container or tank, ideally something like a water butt, into the ground. Set the pump in the tank just beneath the maximum water level so that it is completely submerged. Place a sheet of large-gauge wire-mesh reinforcing over the tank and position the outlet pipes so that they emerge close to the drainage holes in the pots. Then thread the pipes through the drainage holes and secure and waterproof them with an epoxy glue.

Cover the mesh with pebbles, leaving places for aquatic planting baskets to be inserted into the mesh. Arrange the pebbles carefully around and over the baskets so that they are not visible.

There are many plants to choose from, but it is a good idea to have a few creeping specimens, such as *Lysimachia nummularia* 'Aurea', to soften the harshness of the pebbles, and some upright spears of leafy growth to provide contrast. The dwarf variegated *Acorus calamus* 'Variegatus' and *A. gramineus* 'Variegatus' are ideal, as is the common blue-flowered Japanese iris, *Iris laevigata*. Alternatively, *Sagittaria sagittifolia* and *Pontederia cordata* are equally suitable, and likewise *Iris laevigata* 'Colchesteri', with its bold dark purple and white flowers.

PLANTING

1. *Acorus calamus* 'Variegatus'
2. *Acorus gramineus* 'Variegatus'
3. *Iris laevigata*
4. *Lysimachia nummularia* 'Aurea'

Cool but Colourful

This miniature water garden allows you to grow a range of plants in a limited space and combine them with moving water. It is an ideal feature for an open, sunny position on a patio or in a courtyard garden.

This project can be modified to suit your requirements. You can make it a different size, or even in an 'L' shape if you prefer.

- 2 90 cm (36 in) and 2 45 cm (18 in) lengths of 25 cm x 2.5 cm (10 in x 1 in) timber
- 90 cm x 50 cm (36 in x 20 in) piece of 12.5 mm (½ in) exterior plywood
- 2 1 m (40 in) and 2 60 cm (24 in) lengths of decorative moulding
- 2 50 cm (20 in) lengths of split fence post
- Coloured wood preservative
- Panel pins
- 4 plastic corner joints
- Pool liner
- Plastic container (for pump)
- 12.5 mm (½ in) screws
- Hammer, screwdriver, drill, staple gun, sharp knife
- Submersible pump
- Aquatic compost
- Aquatic planting basket
- Fine gravel

◁ **ONE**
Paint the timber with a wood preservative and allow it to dry before tacking the base to the sides with panel pins.

TWO ▷
Secure the top corners with corner joints. Make sure that they will not interfere with the top moulding.

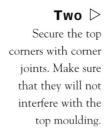

THREE ▷
Attach the split fence posts to the base with screws from the inside. These will raise the container off the ground and allow air to circulate. Then turn the container over and screw the base to the sides.

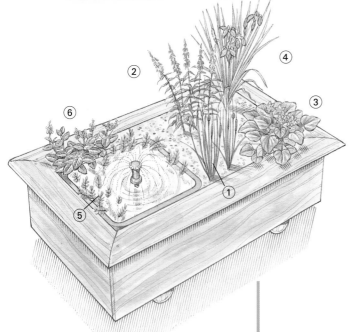

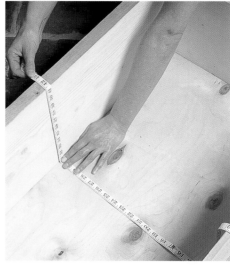

◁ **FOUR**
Measure the box
and prepare the
liner to fit. Make it
slightly larger than
is required.

PLANTING

There are many different plants that
can be used for this project, but you
must curb your enthusiasm and be
careful not to overplant. Any bog
plants used outside the actual water
container will need regular and
generous watering.

① *Typha minima*
② *Lobelia* x *speciosa* 'Queen
   Victoria'
③ *Caltha palustris* 'Flore Pleno'
④ *Iris laevigata*
⑤ *Myriophyllum aquaticum*
⑥ *Veronica beccabunga*

**Alternative plants suitable for
this feature:**
Acorus calamus 'Variegatus'
Primula sikkimensis
Mimulus luteus
Stratiotes aloides
Lobelia x *gerardii* 'Vedrariensis'

◁ **FIVE**
Fit the liner carefully into the
box and attach it with staples.
Trim off any surplus material
with a sharp knife.

SIX ▷
Cut the end of the mouldings at
a 45-degree angle to ensure a
snug fit. Using a fine bit, drill
holes for the screws through the
mouldings. Then hold the
mouldings in position and screw
them securely to the box walls.

SEVEN ▷

In one end, place a waterproof plastic container large enough to accommodate the pump, about 25 cm (10 in) deep. Fill the box around the plastic container with aquatic compost. Alternatively, and more economically, you can fill the lower 15 cm (6 in) of the box with fine gravel and put aquatic compost on top.

◁ EIGHT

Remove the bog plants from their pots and plant them directly into the compost.

△ NINE

When all the bog plants have been put in position within the box, top-dress the surface of the compost with a generous layer of fine gravel. Plant the *Myriophyllum* into a planting basket.

◁ TEN

Position the *Myriophyllum* in the plastic container and fill the latter with water. Place the submersible pump in the container and fix a fountain head to it. The cable should ideally be hidden by some foliage.

Going with the Flow

This feature provides a perfect opportunity to bring moving water to the patio in a natural way. The container is made from timber lined with a pool liner, but any waterproof container of suitable size can be used.

YOU WILL NEED

- Timber box
- Pool liner
- Rocks and/or preformed cascade unit
- Submersible pump
- Aquatic planting basket or large pot with holes
- Stones
- Plastic windbreak netting
- Aquatic compost

Simplicity is the keynote here, since the focus should be on the stone forming the cascade in the centre of this feature. This focal point can be constructed either from pieces of stone, as shown here, or from a preformed cascade unit. Stone works much better in this design and gives the gardener greater freedom to work with the water flow. Be careful what type of stone you choose, since soft materials such as sandstone and freshly quarried limestone can make the water cloudy.

Put the timber box in position and make it watertight with pool liner. Next, place the submersible pump in position and invert a plastic aquatic planting basket or any other large pot with holes over the pump to protect it. Check that the water is deep enough to cover the pump completely, as it must be submerged at all times.

The next step is to erect the stone feature around and over the pump. The way in which the stones are arranged is a matter of personal taste, but ideally the water should emerge from a rocky cascade at one end of the feature and be directed towards the other so that it produces the effect of a small stream. Make the edges of the 'stream' from smaller pieces of rock. Behind these rocks, and disguised by them, place a barrier of plastic windbreak netting, and behind the netting pack in aquatic compost in which to grow your plants. The netting will prevent the compost from spilling into the stream.

Take the plants out of their pots and plant them directly into the compost on either side of the stream. Here, *Iris versicolor* 'Kermesina' and *I. laevigata* 'Rose Queen' have been used to give height, while the marsh marigold, *Caltha palustris*, provides early colour. The careful arrangement of *Calla palustris* softens the rocky edges of the stream.

PLANTING

① *Iris laevigata* 'Rose Queen'
② *Iris versicolor* 'Kermesina'
③ *Caltha palustris*
④ *Calla palustris*

Indoor and Conservatory

Creating water features inside the home is a
relatively recent, but very welcome,
invention. Whether in the living room or
conservatory, the presence of water is a
delight. And not only can you enjoy the
pleasures of water all year round, but the
range of plants you can use is also much
larger due to the more clement conditions.

Spouting Forth

❧

A frog sitting on a lily pad and spouting water entertains everyone, whatever their age. Part of the charm of this feature is the somewhat startled appearance that the vigorous stream of water gives to the frog.

YOU WILL NEED

- Spouting frog
- Terracotta or ceramic container
- Submersible pump
- Aquatic compost
- Aquatic planting baskets
- Large pebbles or cobbles (optional)
- Small pot with holes in the side (optional)
- Large stones (optional)

Gardening should be fun. If we look back through history we see the sort of odd, bizarre and amusing touches – especially in the form of statuary – that prove our gardening ancestors had a sense of humour. This charming frog fountain carries on that tradition.

Any container can be utilised for a fountain such as this, but since the frog is to be the centre of attention, the container should preferably be made from subdued, mellow-coloured terracotta or ceramic. A strongly coloured or busily patterned container will detract from the frog.

Although the frog ornament can be situated anywhere in the container, it is better to put it at the side so that full justice can be done to the spouting water. If you place the frog in the centre of the container, you will have to reduce the pressure on the pump jet so that the water does not splash over the edge. The water can spout into a bowl that contains water, with space for a couple of plants, or the bowl can be filled with pebbles. If you decide on the latter, you must install an inverted pot with holes in the side to create a sump for the pump, and seat the frog and lily pad on top of this arrangement.

Used indoors, such a feature will provide invaluable humidity in a dry atmosphere and it will allow you to plant interesting subtropical marginal plants that might be too tender to plant outdoors, such as the lovely yellow-flowered small arum, *Zantedeschia elliottiana*. This is a superb plant, which contrasts well with the grassy, somewhat filigree foliage of *Cyperus isocladus*. Plant them into aquatic planting baskets filled with aquatic compost, and place them within the container. If necessary, raise the plants on large stones; they should not stand in more than 15 cm (6 in) of water.

① ②

PLANTING

① *Cyperus isocladus*
② *Zantedeschia elliottiana*

Percolating Through

The appeal of this small water feature lies in the feeling of movement, the colour of the wet stone and the attractive ceramic container. Putting it together demands a little care, but it's worth the effort.

YOU WILL NEED

- Ceramic container
- Submersible pump
- Pot with holes in the side
- Discarded tights
- Aquatic compost
- Several large stones
- Large pebbles
- Drilled focal stone

For this feature, situate the pump in the centre of the container and cover it with an inverted pot with holes in the side to allow water to percolate through. This forms a chamber around the pump so that soil and stones cannot interfere with its working.

Place the plants into squares of discarded tights containing aquatic compost. Tights are ideal for this purpose, since they can be cut to size, filled with compost and then tied up, and the plants can be inserted through small holes cut in the fabric. The fine weave of the tights prevents compost from seeping out and polluting the water, and it is also very flexible and moulds easily to the spaces around the pump chamber. It is important in such a restricted space that you choose plants whose root systems will adapt to such constraints.

It is a good idea to wedge the pump chamber with two or three large stones before inserting the plants. Position the plants and place fairly large pebbles around and over the top of the planting bags to disguise them completely. The main focal stone, which you can buy ready-drilled, is then positioned on the top and the outlet of the pump fed into it. Use a main stone of sandstone or limestone, but make sure that it is well weathered and has a hard outer coat so that the water does not gradually erode it and produce a gritty deposit that may get into the pump. Freshly quarried stone often looks bright and clean, but may wear away quickly.

Use a combination of plants with an upright habit for this feature, but include at least one scrambling plant such as the parrot feather, *Myriophyllum aquaticum*, to hide the edge. The best plants for introducing a little height and character are the double-flowered arrowhead, *Sagittaria sagittaria* 'Flore Pleno', the corkscrew rush, *Juncus effusus* 'Spiralis', and *Typha minima*. All of these plants are very attractive when grown together and cope well in restricted growing conditions.

PLANTING

① *Juncus effusus* 'Spiralis'
② *Myriophyllum aquaticum*
③ *Typha minima*
④ *Sagittaria sagittifolia*
   'Flore Pleno'

Music and Movement

This is an attractive, ready-made indoor water feature where the water flows gently around and across the metal leaves. For the best effect, place it in a well-lit position or focus a spotlight on it.

You Will Need

- Ready-made water feature with metal leaves
- Crushed charcoal (filter carbon)
- Aquatic compost
- Discarded tights
- Artificial plants (optional)

This feature contains a discreet pump that you merely have to plug in and switch on to start working. Although it is very striking left plain, plants set in the bowl will help to soften the effect.

A small indoor feature like this will lose a considerable amount of moisture through evaporation, so you need to top it up regularly with fresh water. In order to prevent the water from becoming stale, add a tablespoonful of fine charcoal such as that used in aquarium filters, which is known as filter carbon. In such a small volume of water, particularly where it is constantly moving, it is difficult to raise water quality by introducing submerged plants. While they would thrive, they would almost certainly become an unsightly tangle. In this feature, the container has been filled with attractive pebbles to complement the plants, give it additional stability and help to overcome potential problems with water clarity.

There are few tender plants that occupy little space and can be used to dress a bowl, but varieties of *Acorus gramineus* and the dwarf-growing *Cyperus isocladus* are perfect for the job. However, they need careful preparation and placement. Fortunately, these plants can exist with a very modest amount of growing medium, and by wrapping the roots of each plant in a generous handful of aquatic compost in an old pair of tights and securing it firmly you can fit the plants into the bowl without causing any spillage or polluting the water.

In the case of small indoor features such as this one, it is worth considering artificial plants. Good-quality ones are not affected by the water or temperature and can be used in awkward places. Here, artificial ivy has been twined around the stems of the metal leaves to give the feature an attractive, more natural appearance.

Planting

1. *Acorus gramineus* 'Ogon'
2. *Cyperus isocladus*

Terrific for the Sideboard

❧

This is more a humidifier than a water feature but, if a deep enough bowl is selected, there is no reason why it cannot be turned into a miniature water garden.

You Will Need

- Ceramic or terracotta bowl
- Submersible pump
- Small pot with holes in the side
- Pebbles
- Drilled focal stone
- Crushed charcoal (filter carbon)
- Aquatic compost
- Discarded tights

This type of feature is often referred to as a tabletop fountain, although where there is access all around the table this can cause a problem, since there is an electric cable that must be disguised. It is better used as a sideboard decoration, where the wire can be tucked discreetly out of sight.

Position the pump in a small chamber. This can easily be created from an upturned pot that has holes in the side through which the water can pass. Pack well-washed pebbles around the chamber to disguise it. On top of this, set the waterfall stone, which has a hole drilled in the upper part through which the pump outlet is installed. The top layer of pebbles is very important, as it can enhance this feature visually or make it look quite ordinary. The pebbles should be of roughly equal size and of a colour that pleasingly echoes the colour of the central waterfall stone. Adding a little charcoal to the water will keep it sweet and clear. Use a tablespoonful of crushed charcoal, such as that sold as filter carbon for aquariums. This should overcome any odour problems and reduces possible discoloration of the pebbles by algae.

Choose dwarf-growing plants, such as the varieties of *Acorus gramineus* and the diminutive *Cyperus isocladus*, and establish them in aquatic compost wrapped up in pieces of discarded tights. *Pleioblastus pygmaeus* is an excellent alternative for planting this feature.

During the winter months ensure that the plants receive sufficient light. When kept in a well-lit position, they will remain evergreen and in character. If they do not make it through the winter, you would do best to dispose of them and replant the feature in the spring.

Planting

① *Acorus gramineus* 'Variegatus'

② *Cyperus isocladus*

Raising the Sights

❧

The simple planting and the rustic construction of this pool provide the focal point in a more colourful planted area. The water flowing over the rocky cascade brings a touch of the countryside to the conservatory.

YOU WILL NEED

This project can be adjusted to any size. Since it will be quite heavy when completed, it is better to build larger constructions *in situ*.

- 6 45 cm x 30 cm (18 in x 12 in) pieces of 12.5 mm (½ in) exterior plywood
- 2 hexagons of 12.5 mm (½ in) exterior plywood with 45 cm (18 in) sides
- 30 45 cm (18 in) lengths of 7.5 cm x 2.5 cm (3 in x 1 in) fencing rails
- 24 plastic corner joints
- 12.5 mm (½ in) and 2.5 cm (1 in) screws
- Nails (optional)
- Wood preservative, clear and coloured
- Cascade waterfall unit
- Pool liner
- Submersible pump
- Screwdriver, staple gun, jigsaw, drill, hammer (optional)
- Aquatic compost
- Aquatic planting baskets
- Fine gravel
- Bricks or aquatic planting baskets

◁ ONE

Place the hexagonal base on the floor and screw the sides on to it, using 12 corner joints and 12.5 mm (½ in) screws.

TWO ▷

Position the waterfall unit on the top hexagon and draw around it. Leave about 4 cm (1½ in) of wood around the edge and a crossbar to support the feature. Cut out this shape and the rest of the internal hexagon with a jigsaw.

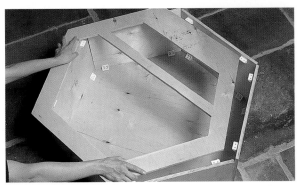

◁ THREE

Screw the other 12 corner joints in place around the top and then screw the top hexagon into position, using 12.5 mm (½ in) screws.

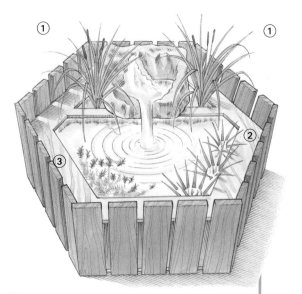

PLANTING

The success of this design depends largely upon its rustic appearance and the simplicity of moving water, so few plants are used. For the best effect, position two graceful-looking flowering plants of the same kind on either side of the cascade unit. Alternatively, you could have sentinel-like plants such as *Iris laevigata* varieties, which would give it a more sculptural appearance. You could add a floating aquatic plant, but avoid a carpeting type such as azolla. Submerged aquatics, such as *Myriophyllum aquaticum*, are an optional extra.

① *Carex elata* 'Bowles' Golden'
② *Stratiotes aloides*
③ *Myriophyllum aquaticum*

◁ **FOUR**
To add strength, screw the sides directly into the top and base with 2.5cm (1 in) screws. Then paint the whole construction with clear wood preservative.

FIVE ▷
Paint the rails with coloured wood preservative and secure them with 2.5 cm (1 in) screws.

◁ **SIX**
Cut the pool liner to shape and insert it carefully into the pool. Fasten it to the underside of the top hexagon with a staple gun.

◁ SEVEN

Site the
completed
container, ready
for planting,
in a sunny
spot in your
conservatory.

EIGHT ▷

Remove the plants
carefully from their
pots and place them
in aquatic planting
baskets filled with
aquatic compost.
Cover the surfaces
with fine gravel.
Position them in the
container, bringing
them up to the right
level by standing
them on inverted
planting baskets or
bricks.

▽ NINE

Once the plants are in place you can secure the cascade unit by drilling
a hole into the base of the unit and screwing it to the top hexagon.
Drill another hole in the back of the unit for the pump outlet.

△ TEN

Position the pump in the
container and connect the pump
outlet to the cascade unit
through the drilled hole, and the
cable to the electrical supply. Fill
the pool with water.

Going Potty

The herb cluster pot is a popular element in container water gardens. These united terracotta pots are perfect for a moving water feature for indoors, or for a temporary summer arrangement outside.

YOU WILL NEED

- Large decorative bowl
- Submersible pump
- Large pot with holes in the side, or fine-gauge wire-mesh reinforcing
- Terracotta herb cluster pots
- Pebbles
- Aquatic compost
- Discarded tights
- Artificial plants (optional)

The large bowl in this feature serves as a reservoir for the pump, which is placed on the bottom. Protect the pump by enclosing it in a large inverted pot with holes in the side, through which the outlet hose passes and water can flow back in. Alternatively, you can use screwed-up fine-gauge wire-mesh reinforcing. It may not look particularly strong, but in sufficient quantity it forms a sound base on which to place the surface pebbles and the terracotta herb cluster pots. To connect the pots to the pump, fix a small plastic insert into the base of the centre pot and push the outlet hose from the submersible pump on to it.

Grow the plants in aquatic compost wrapped in securely knotted pieces of old tights. This allows the plants to develop their own rootballs without the compost discolouring the water. You can then mould the rootballs into the space available and place pebbles around the base of the plants to cover them up.

The plants used in this feature are a combination of fairly tender and suitable hardy kinds. *Cyperus isocladus* is a tropical plant that can stand quite cool temperatures. *Acorus gramineus* 'Ogon' is hardy, but suffers if winters are severe, while the scrambling *Lysimachia nummularia* 'Aurea' is completely hardy. With such a plant combination you need to be careful to maintain the correct temperature, as too much warmth, especially in the absence of good light, leads to distorted growth. If winter conditions indoors are too dull and the plants appear to suffer, remove them completely and replant the feature in the spring.

Although no self-respecting gardener would normally wish to use artificial plants, in instances where a water feature appears stark without green foliage there are good reasons for experimenting with some of the high-quality artificial specimens that are now available. In poor growing conditions, where live plants suffer, this may be the best solution.

PLANTING

1. *Acorus gramineus* 'Ogon'
2. *Cyperus isocladus*
3. *Lysimachia nummularia* 'Aurea'

Corner Piece

This movable water feature is an ideal way to bring water into a conservatory. It can be used with a fountain jet, but is equally attractive as a planted feature without moving water.

YOU WILL NEED

This project can be adapted to suit almost any situation. It is a simple matter to make it deeper or longer. In this instance, it is small enough to be easily portable.

- 1.2 m x 1.2 m (48 in x 48 in) square of 12.5 mm (½ in) exterior plywood, cut diagonally to create two triangles
- 2 1.2 m x 30 cm (48 in x 12 in), and 1 1.72 m x 30 cm (69 in x 12 in) lengths of 12.5 mm (½ in) exterior plywood
- 1.72 m (69 in) length of decorative moulding
- 2 90 cm (36 in) lengths of trellis
- 12 plastic corner joints
- 5 cm (2 in) and 2.5 mm (½ in) screws
- Glue
- Panel pins
- Coloured wood preservative
- Pool liner
- Hammer, screwdriver, drill, jigsaw
- Aquatic compost
- Aquatic planting baskets
- Fine gravel
- Bricks or aquatic planting baskets

ONE ▷
Screw and glue the front and sides to the base, using 12 corner joints and 12.5 mm (½ in) screws.

△ **TWO**
With a jigsaw, cut the shape of the pond out of the upper triangle, leaving a 15-cm (6-in) wide shelf all around for pot plants.

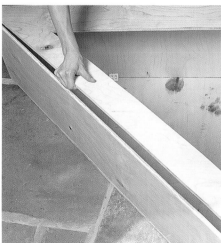

◁ **THREE**
Apply glue around the top rim of the sides, and position the upper triangle on top.

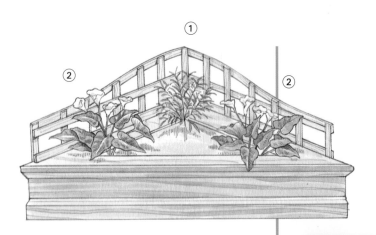

① *Pleioblastus pygmaeus*
② *Zantedeschia aethiopica*

FOUR ▷
Pin the top securely
into position using
panel pins.

PLANTING

Only a limited number of aquatic
plants can be used in a pool of this
kind, since most tropical plants grow
too big and boisterous to be suitable.
Apart from aquatic plants, you can
use decorative indoor plants on the
shelves to create an ever-changing
display. Most plants will benefit from
the localised humidity created by the
pool. If you use plants that tolerate
low light levels, this feature can be
kept indoors.

① *Pleioblastus pygmaeus*
② *Zantedeschia aethiopica*

**Alternative plants suitable for this
feature:**
Cyperus isocladus
Zantedeschia elliottiana

◁ **FIVE**
Paint the whole
container with
wood preservative
and allow to dry.
Then attach the
moulding to the
front edges of the
pool with screws
from the inside.

SIX ▷
Pre-drill holes in the trellis to
prevent the wood from
splitting, and screw the two
lengths to the back of the pool
to form a corner.

Seven ▷

Cut the pool liner slightly larger than required and arrange it carefully by hand. Staple it underneath the inside edge of the pool and trim off the surplus.

△ **Eight**

The pool is now ready for planting. Use bricks or inverted planting baskets as supports in the corners where you are planning to place the plants.

▽ **Nine**

Plant the aquatic plants in planting baskets filled with aquatic compost, and cover their tops with fine gravel. Carefully place the baskets on their supports in the pool.

Ten ▷

Add water to the pool, taking care not to disturb the plants.

Directory of Plants

This directory is not exhaustive, but offers a wide range of planting suggestions for container water gardening. Your choices will be governed by the shape of your container and, in the case of an outdoor feature, by climatic considerations. The plants described here are largely trouble-free to grow and will not swamp the confined conditions of small containers.

How to Use the Directory

The plants in the Directory are listed·alphabetically by their Latin names. All the information you need about the plant is contained under the headings described below and opposite. Numerous varieties of aquatic plants are suitable for container water gardens; those selected here are the best for the widest range of climates and conditions.

The moisture-loving Primula beesiana.

When purchasing aquatic plants, be sure that they are nursery grown. A considerable number of the plants that are available more cheaply have been removed from the wild and are not only traded illegally, but are more difficult to establish. They can also introduce undesirable pests and diseases into your water feature.

① **Botanical name** is international and the form given here is the one usually used in nurseries and garden centres.

② **Common name** is the name used by most people to refer to the plant.

③ **Minimum temperature** is the lowest temperature at which a plant can survive. It is important to remember that this is only a guide. A plant's ability to survive certain temperatures is also affected by factors like protection from the wind.

④ **Zone** Each plant has a number or range of numbers that corresponds with the hardiness zone maps on pages 114–15.

⑤ **Characteristics** describes the general growth habit and both foliage and flowers of the plant, together with the expected height in a single season. Measurements for floating aquatic plants and deep-water aquatics such as waterlilies represent their spread across the surface of the water.

⑥ **Cultivation** gives details of specific requirements, along with notes on propagation.

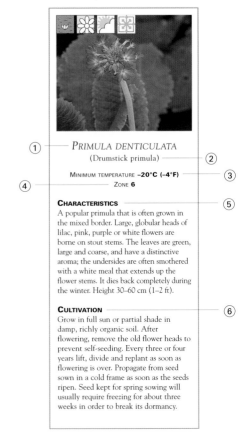

① *PRIMULA DENTICULATA*
② (Drumstick primula)

③ MINIMUM TEMPERATURE **–20°C (–4°F)**
④ ZONE **6**

⑤ **CHARACTERISTICS**
A popular primula that is often grown in the mixed border. Large, globular heads of lilac, pink, purple or white flowers are borne on stout stems. The leaves are green, large and coarse, and have a distinctive aroma; the undersides are often smothered with a white meal that extends up the flower stems. It dies back completely during the winter. Height 30–60 cm (1–2 ft).

⑥ **CULTIVATION**
Grow in full sun or partial shade in damp, richly organic soil. After flowering, remove the old flower heads to prevent self-seeding. Every three or four years lift, divide and replant as soon as flowering is over. Propagate from seed sown in a cold frame as soon as the seeds ripen. Seed kept for spring sowing will usually require freezing for about three weeks in order to break its dormancy.

SYMBOLS AT THE TOP OF EACH PLANT ENTRY GIVE THE FOLLOWING INFORMATION AT A GLANCE:

 Deep-water aquatics are plants, such as waterlilies, that grow on the floor of the pool or water feature and produce leaves that float on the surface of the water. Although described as deep-water aquatics, they do tolerate the shallows of a container water feature. The difference is that they do not produce aerial foliage.

Marginal plants usually grow in the water at the edge of a pool. They tolerate standing water or very wet conditions all year round. They are the most important group of plants for container water features.

Bog plants differ from marginal plants in that they will not tolerate standing water, especially during the winter. They require very damp soil.

Floating plants are aquatics that float around freely on the surface of the water. They derive their nourishment from the water and often sink and take the form of a turion or winter bud in the autumn.

Submerged plants grow completely beneath the water, although they may produce flowers on the surface. It is these plants that help to keep the water clear and sweet.

Flowering period (if applicable)

Spring   *Summer*   *Autumn*   *Cross-seasonal*

 Weediness These plants may be classified as weeds in some countries. Weediness indicates that a particular plant, if left to its own devices, may swamp its less vigorous neighbours. It will therefore need regular cutting back. There is also the danger that, if allowed to escape into the wild, it will become a nuisance.

 Winter hardiness This denotes the degree of cold that a plant will tolerate before it is damaged. Occasionally, if there are variations of cold and relative warmth during the winter months, a plant may succumb at a higher temperature, as it may be induced to start growing before being hit by cold weather again.

Full sun Requires full sun.

Light shade Tolerates light shade.

The striking orchid primula, Primula vialii.

ACORUS CALAMUS 'VARIEGATUS'
(Variegated sweet flag)

MINIMUM TEMPERATURE **–15°C (5°F)**
ZONE **7**

CHARACTERISTICS
Very hardy marginal plant with cream, green and rose-flushed, boldly variegated, sword-shaped, irislike leaves. These have a strong tangerine fragrance if bruised. The first shoots in spring take on a bright crimson hue and grow from fat, fleshy rhizomes. The insignificant yellowish green hornlike flower spikes appear among the foliage in midsummer. Height 90–120 cm (3–4 ft).

CULTIVATION
Grow in moist soil or up to 5 cm (2 in) of water in an open, sunny position. Propagate by dividing the fleshy rhizomes during the active growing season. Plant only vigorous young fans of leaves. Discard old woody rhizomes.

ACORUS GRAMINEUS 'MINIMUS'

MINIMUM TEMPERATURE **–6°C (21°F)**
ZONE **9**

CHARACTERISTICS
Semi-evergreen, marginal plant with small, grassy, deep green leaves. Insignificant hornlike flower spikes are occasionally produced among the foliage during summer. In frost-free conditions, the plant is evergreen. If temperatures fall below freezing, it dies back or, in many instances, disappears completely, especially when in standing water. Height up to 8 cm (3 in).

CULTIVATION
Grow in moist soil or up to 2 cm (¾ in) of water in an open, sunny position. Grows best in a frost-free environment in a greenhouse or conservatory with a minimum temperature of about 13°C (55°F). Propagate by dividing established plants during spring or early autumn.

ACORUS GRAMINEUS 'OGON'

MINIMUM TEMPERATURE **–6°C (21°F)**
ZONE **9**

CHARACTERISTICS
Semi-evergreen, marginal plant with small, narrow irislike leaves, which are variegated with chartreuse and cream. The tiny hornlike flower spikes are produced sparingly among the foliage in midsummer, but are rarely noticed. In frost-free conditions, the plant is evergreen, responding well to subtropical temperatures. If temperatures fall below freezing, it dies back to its small wiry creeping rhizome and does not reappear until the following spring. Height up to 10 cm (4 in).

CULTIVATION
Grow in moist soil or in up to 2 cm (¾ in) of water in an open, sunny position or, preferably, in a greenhouse where the minimum temperature is 13°C (55°F). Propagate by dividing established plants during spring or early autumn.

ACORUS GRAMINEUS 'VARIEGATUS'
(Variegated dwarf sweet flag)

MINIMUM TEMPERATURE **–6°C (21°F)**
ZONE **9**

CHARACTERISTICS
Semi-evergreen, variegated, marginal plant with small, narrow irislike leaves, strikingly variegated with dark green and cream. The small hornlike flowers are insignificant and are noticed only by the most observant gardener. In frost-free conditions, the plant remains lush and evergreen. When temperatures fall below freezing, it often dies back to its tiny rhizome and reappears the following spring. Height up to 10 cm (4 in).

CULTIVATION
Grow in moist soil or in up to 2 cm (¾ in) of water in an open, sunny position. Although fairly hardy, it is best cultivated in subtropical conditions at a temperature of about 13°C (55°F). Propagate by dividing established clumps during spring or early autumn.

ALISMA LANCEOLATUM
(Narrow-leafed water plantain)

MINIMUM TEMPERATURE **–20°C (–4°F)**
ZONE **6**

CHARACTERISTICS
Very hardy marginal plant with dark green, lance-shaped or elliptical leaves arising in neat, nonspreading clumps. The slender branched spires of pink three-petalled flowers are produced in midsummer. The plant dies back completely during the winter. Height 40–60 cm (16–24 in).

CULTIVATION
Grow in moist soil or in up to 15 cm (6 in) of water in an open, sunny position. As soon as flowering is over, remove the faded flower spikes, since these will set seed that will spread freely and the plant can become a nuisance. Propagate by dividing established clumps of plants during spring, or from seed sown as soon as the seeds ripen.

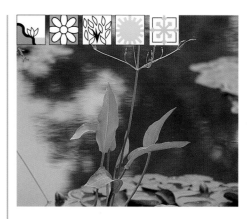

ALISMA PLANTAGO-AQUATICA
(Water plantain)

MINIMUM TEMPERATURE **–20°C (–4°F)**
ZONE **6**

CHARACTERISTICS
Very hardy marginal plant which grows in neat clumps. The bright green, oval leaves are held upright above the water, and loose, pyramidal spires of white or pinkish papery flowers are produced among them. Once flowering is over, the old flower heads become woody and are often harvested and dried for indoor decoration. The plant dies down completely during the winter. Height 60–90 cm (2–3 ft).

CULTIVATION
Grow in moist soil or in up to 15 cm (6 in) of water in an open, sunny position. To prevent unwanted seeding, remove old flower stems as soon as the flowers have faded. Propagate by dividing the plants in spring, or from seed sown as soon as the seeds ripen.

APONOGETON DISTACHYOS
(Water hawthorn)

MINIMUM TEMPERATURE **–15°C (5°F)**
ZONE **7**

CHARACTERISTICS
Submerged aquatic plant with floating
foliage. The leaves are roughly
rectangular with rounded ends and are
dark olive green, splashed sparingly with
maroon or deep purple. The flowers,
which are held just above the water, are
forked and consist of two white, bractlike
organs with black stamens. They are
produced throughout the summer and
have a strong vanilla fragrance. Spread
45–60 cm (18–24 in).

CULTIVATION
Grow in full sun in 30–90 cm (1–3 ft)
of water. Plant in a soil-based compost,
ideally in a small aquatic planting basket.
Propagate by dividing established plants
during early spring, or by sowing seeds in
pots of saturated heavy soil while they
are still green.

ASTILBE x CRISPA 'PERKEO'

MINIMUM TEMPERATURE **–20°C (–4°F)**
ZONE **6**

CHARACTERISTICS
Hardy, dwarf, moisture-loving perennial
with handsome, much-divided, bronze-
green leaves. Feathery plumes of deep
pink flowers are produced in mid- to late
summer. A clump-forming plant that dies
down completely for the winter months.
Height 20 cm (8 in).

CULTIVATION
Grow in a moisture-retaining, richly
organic soil in a sunny position. Although
astilbe will tolerate occasional inundation
with water, it grows best in moist soil
rather than in standing water. Remove
the old flower spikes as soon as flowering
finishes. Propagate by dividing the woody
crowns during autumn or in early spring.

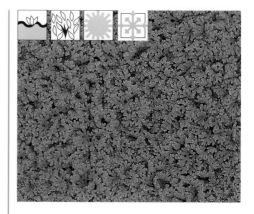

AZOLLA CAROLINIANA
(Fairy moss)

MINIMUM TEMPERATURE **–15°C (5°F)**
ZONE **7**

CHARACTERISTICS
Spreading, floating fern with delicate
green foliage, often with a purplish tinge.
The individual plantlets are about 1 cm
(⅜ in) tall and up to 1 cm (⅜ in) across.
In bright sunshine and at the approach of
autumn it frequently takes on a strong
reddish hue.

CULTIVATION
Grow in an open, sunny position,
preferably in slightly alkaline water. A
free-floating plant, fairy moss does not
take severe weather well. As a precaution
against winter damage in cold areas,
remove a portion of the fronds towards
the end of the growing season and place
it in a bowl of water with a little soil at
the bottom in a light, frost-free place.
This will encourage early growth the
following spring. Propagate by separating
and redistributing groups of foliage.

BUTOMUS UMBELLATUS
(Flowering rush)

MINIMUM TEMPERATURE **–25°C (–13°F)**
ZONE **5**

CHARACTERISTICS

Hardy, elegant, rushlike, marginal plant with narrow, bright green, slightly twisted foliage which grows in neat clumps. Spreading, showy umbels of bright rose pink flowers are produced during late summer. A white-flowered form is also available. The plant dies back and becomes completely dormant during the winter. Height 60–90 cm (2–3 ft).

CULTIVATION

Grow in moist soil or in up to 23 cm (9 in) of water in an open, sunny position. Remove the old flower stems as they fade. If waterlily aphids infest the plants, knock them off with a strong stream of water from a hose. Propagate by removing bulbils from the base of mature plants in early spring, or by dividing established clumps during the growing season.

CALLA PALUSTRIS
(Bog arum)

MINIMUM TEMPERATURE **–30°C (–22°F)**
ZONE **4**

CHARACTERISTICS

A marginal plant which flowers in late spring or early summer. The small, white sail-like flowers are replaced by bright orange-red fruits during late summer and early autumn. A scrambling plant, it produces strong, creeping stems that are densely clothed with bright green, glossy, heart-shaped leaves. Height 15–30 cm (6–12 in).

CULTIVATION

Grow in an open, sunny position in moist soil or in up to 5 cm (2 in) of water. Plants soon become untidy, so they should be lifted each spring and the young growths separated out and replanted. Propagate either from seed sown as soon as the seeds ripen, or from short sections of creeping stem, each with a bud, inserted into trays of saturated heavy soil.

CALTHA LEPTOSEPALA
(Mountain marigold)

MINIMUM TEMPERATURE **–35°C (–31°F)**
ZONE **3**

CHARACTERISTICS

Small-growing, marginal plant of neat habit, which produces a mound of dark green, scalloped foliage which is pleasing even when the plant is not in flower. Broad, white, saucer-shaped flowers are produced during late spring and early summer. The plant dies back completely in the winter months. Height 15–45 cm (6–18 in).

CULTIVATION

Grow in a sunny position in moist soil or in up to 5 cm (2 in) of water. Remove faded flower heads. Lift and divide plants every second year in order to maintain vigour. Propagate by dividing the plants after flowering, or from seed sown in pots of saturated heavy soil as soon as the seeds ripen.

CALTHA PALUSTRIS
(Marsh marigold)

MINIMUM TEMPERATURE **–35°C (–31°F)**
ZONE **3**

CHARACTERISTICS
Lovely early-flowering, marginal plant. Very hardy, with neat, dark green mounds of scalloped foliage and bright golden yellow, waxy flowers. 'Alba' has smaller white flowers with yellow centres, 'Flore Pleno' has bright golden, fully double flowers on neater-growing plants. It dies back completely during the winter months. Height 30–60 cm (1–2 ft).

CULTIVATION
Grow in moist soil or up to 30 cm (12 in) of water in a sunny position. In summer, mildew and fungal infections may occur, disfiguring the foliage. Treat badly affected plants with a systemic fungicide, and remove faded flowers and deteriorating leaves. Propagate by dividing established plants during spring, or from seed sown in pots of saturated heavy soil as soon as the seeds ripen.

CAREX ELATA 'BOWLES' GOLDEN' (syn. *C. elata* 'Aurea') (Golden tufted sedge)

MINIMUM TEMPERATURE **–15°C (5°F)**
ZONE **7**

CHARACTERISTICS
Most attractive bog garden sedge which has coarse, grassy, bright golden foliage with narrow green edges. During the summer, insignificant tufts of flowers are produced which are generally removed to preserve the quality of the foliage. Clump-forming, and in mild winters remaining more or less evergreen. Height 40–60 cm (16–24 in).

CULTIVATION
Prefers an open, sunny position in damp soil. Does not enjoy standing in water during the winter. The best golden colour is produced when the soil is poor – a high level of nutrients tends to encourage pale green foliage. Propagate by dividing established plants during early spring.

CERATOPHYLLUM DEMERSUM
(Hornwort)

MINIMUM TEMPERATURE **–10°C (14°F)**
ZONE **8**

CHARACTERISTICS
Totally submerged aquatic plant with whorls of dark green, needlelike, bristly foliage on slender, brittle stems. In early spring, these are sometimes temporarily rooted to the pool floor, but for most of the year are completely free, floating just beneath the surface of the water. Individual shoots can grow up to 30 cm (1 ft). In winter the plant disperses as turions, or winter buds, reappearing when the water warms up again in spring.

CULTIVATION
A most adaptable, submerged aquatic plant for full sun or partial shade. Although it is normally introduced to a water feature as a bunched plant, it rarely roots and is usually allowed to grow largely unrestricted beneath the water surface. Propagate by separating and redistributing the branched stems.

CYPERUS ISOCLADUS
(syn. C. 'Haspan')
(Miniature papyrus)

MINIMUM TEMPERATURE **0°C (32°F)**
ZONE **10**

CHARACTERISTICS
A miniature version of the famous
Egyptian papyrus for small-pool
cultivation indoors. An elegant plant
with stout stems that give rise to
umbrellalike heads of very fine, bright
green foliage. Insignificant brownish
flowers are produced. When grown in
warm conditions of at least 15°C (59°F),
it remains completely evergreen. Height
60–90 cm (2–3 ft).

CULTIVATION
A marginal plant tolerating conditions
from moist soil up to 15 cm (6 in) of
water. It is happy in full sun or partial
shade and is easily increased by division
during the active growing season. It is
best grown with a minimum night
temperature of 15°C (59°F).

EGERIA DENSA
(syn. *Elodea densa*)

MINIMUM TEMPERATURE **–5°C (23°F)**
ZONE **9**

CHARACTERISTICS
Totally submerged aquatic plant of similar
appearance to, and often confused with,
the very hardy goldfish weed (*Lagarosiphon
major*). Dark green, firm leaflets are carried
in dense whorls around strong, green,
scrambling stems. The flowers are
insignificant. A very popular plant with
fish keepers, it is reliably evergreen when
maintained above freezing.

CULTIVATION
Ideally grow with a minimum water
temperature of 10°C (50°F) in order to
maintain a lush, well-clothed appearance.
Clumps of the plant should be rooted
into a container on the floor of the water
feature. Propagate from short stem
cuttings taken during the active growing
season and fastened together with a twist
tie. Plant these bunches in their
permanent positions.

ELEOCHARIS ACICULARIS
(Hairgrass, Needle spike-rush)

MINIMUM TEMPERATURE **–15°C (5°F)**
ZONE **7**

CHARACTERISTICS
Totally submerged aquatic plant which
looks rather like a carpet of grass,
although it is in no way related to that
group of plants. In fact, it is a close
relative of the rushes and sedges. An
evergreen plant which produces bright
green foliage even in freezing conditions.
Height up to 20 cm (8 in).

CULTIVATION
The perfect submerged aquatic plant
for tub or sink gardening, since it grows
in a restrained clump-forming fashion.
Although very hardy, it also responds well
to tropical conditions. Propagate by
dividing the clumps. Unlike most other
submerged plants, cuttings will not root.

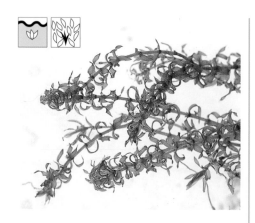

ELODEA CANADENSIS
(Canadian pondweed)

MINIMUM TEMPERATURE **−20°C (−4°F)**
ZONE **6**

CHARACTERISTICS
This handsome and widely cultivated aquatic remains completely submerged. Small, dark green leaves are arranged in very dense whorls along extensive branching stems. Unless the weather is very severe, elodea usually remains evergreen and is much liked by fish.

CULTIVATION
Elodea canadensis has a reputation for being invasive, but it is easily contained if restricted to a planter. Although evergreen, it should ideally be replaced with fresh cuttings from early spring growth each year. These should be gathered together and secured with a twist tie before planting. This is also the method for propagation.

HOSTA FORTUNEI 'GOLD STANDARD'

MINIMUM TEMPERATURE **−20°C (−4°F)**
ZONE **6**

CHARACTERISTICS
Perennial bog plant with heavily textured, golden, rounded leaves edged with dark green. Although grown primarily as a foliage plant, it produces spikes of pendent, pale lavender, bell-like flowers in midsummer. Hostas die back at the first sign of frost, disappearing completely for the winter. Height 40–60 cm (16–24 in).

CULTIVATION
Grow in a wet, richly organic soil, but not in standing water, in either sun or partial shade. Protect from attack by slugs early in the growing season. Propagate by dividing established clumps during early spring. At this time, if carefully lifted with a fork, the root clump should separate easily.

HOSTA PLANTAGINEA
(August lily)

MINIMUM TEMPERATURE **−20°C (−4°F)**
ZONE **6**

CHARACTERISTICS
Perennial bog plant which has glossy green leaves with conspicuous veins and wavy margins. Although grown primarily as a foliage plant, it produces spikes of fragrant, pendent, white tubular flowers in midsummer. Hostas die back at the first sign of frost, disappearing completely for the winter. Height 40–60 cm (16–24 in).

CULTIVATION
Grow in a wet, richly organic soil, but not in standing water, in sun or partial shade. Protect from attack by slugs early in the growing season. Propagate by dividing established clumps during early spring. At this time, lift the plant carefully with a fork and the root clump will separate easily.

HOSTA SIEBOLDIANA 'ELEGANS'

MINIMUM TEMPERATURE **–20°C (–4°F)**
ZONE **6**

CHARACTERISTICS
Perennial bog plant which has beautiful steely blue, oval leaves with a ribbed and corrugated surface. Although grown primarily as a foliage plant, it produces strong spikes of handsome, pale lilac or slightly off-white tubular flowers in midsummer. Hostas die back at the first sign of frost, disappearing completely for the winter. Height 40–60 cm (16–24 in).

CULTIVATION
Grow in a wet, richly organic soil, but not in standing water, in sun or partial shade. Protect from attack by slugs early in the growing season. Propagate by dividing established clumps during early spring. At this time, lift the plant carefully with a fork and the root clump will separate easily.

HOSTA SIEBOLDIANA 'FRANCES WILLIAMS'

MINIMUM TEMPERATURE **–20°C (–4°F)**
ZONE **6**

CHARACTERISTICS
Perennial bog plant which has beautiful blue-green, ribbed leaves with beige edges. Although grown primarily as a foliage plant, it produces strong spikes of pendent, pale lilac or off-white tubular flowers in midsummer. Hostas die back at the first sign of frost, disappearing completely for the winter. Height 40–60 cm (16–24 in).

CULTIVATION
Grow in a wet, richly organic soil, but not in standing water, in either sun or partial shade. Protect from attack by slugs early in the growing season. Propagate by dividing established clumps during early spring. At this time, if carefully lifted with a fork, the root clump should separate easily.

HOSTA 'THOMAS HOGG'

MINIMUM TEMPERATURE **–20°C (–4°F)**
ZONE **6**

CHARACTERISTICS
Perennial bog plant which has large, bold, green leaves with a distinctive white margin. Although grown primarily as a foliage plant, it produces spikes of slender, pendent, lilac tubular flowers during midsummer. Hostas die back at the first sign of frost, disappearing completely for the winter. Height 25–40 cm (10–16 in).

CULTIVATION
Grow in a wet, richly organic soil, but not in standing water, in either sun or partial shade. Protect from attack by slugs early in the growing season. Propagate by dividing established clumps during early spring. At this time, if carefully lifted with a fork, the root clump should separate easily.

HOSTA UNDULATA 'MEDIO-VARIEGATA'

MINIMUM TEMPERATURE **–20°C (–4°F)**
ZONE **6**

CHARACTERISTICS
Perennial bog plant which has
undulating, lance-shaped, cream and
green variegated leaves. Although grown
primarily as a foliage plant, it produces
narrow spikes of slender, pendent, lilac
bell-like flowers during midsummer.
Hostas die back at the first sign of frost,
disappearing completely for the winter.
Height 25–40 cm (10–16 in).

CULTIVATION
Grow in a wet, richly organic soil, but
not in standing water, in either sun or
partial shade. Protect from attack by
slugs early in the growing season.
Propagate by dividing established clumps
during early spring. At this time, if
carefully lifted with a fork, the root
clump should separate easily.

HOSTA VENTRICOSA

MINIMUM TEMPERATURE **–20°C (–4°F)**
ZONE **6**

CHARACTERISTICS
Perennial bog plant with narrow and
slightly undulating, bright green leaves.
Although grown primarily as a foliage
plant, it produces spikes of attractive,
pendent, deep lilac-mauve tubular
flowers in midsummer. Hostas die back
at the first sign of frost, disappearing
completely for the winter. Height
30–50 cm (12–20 in).

CULTIVATION
Grow in a wet, richly organic soil, but
not in standing water, in either sun or
partial shade. Protect from attack by
slugs early in the growing season.
Propagate by dividing established clumps
during early spring. At this time, if
carefully lifted with a fork, the root
clump should separate easily.

HOUTTUYNIA CORDATA 'CHAMELEON'
(syn. *H. cordata* 'Variegata')

MINIMUM TEMPERATURE **–25°C (–13°F)**
ZONE **5**

CHARACTERISTICS
Bog garden perennial with beautiful
yellow, red, purple and green variegated
foliage. Although hardy to Zone 5, this
plant does require careful siting, since the
young shoots are vulnerable to frost
damage. The roughly heart-shaped leaves
have an unpleasant odour if bruised.
Small, creamy white, cone-shaped flowers
are produced sparingly during the summer.
The whole plant dies back completely for
the winter. Height 15–30 cm (6–12 in).

CULTIVATION
Choose a moist soil in a sunny position.
Although houttuynias will grow in up to
5 cm (2 in) of water, they do best when
grown in wet soil. Propagate by division
once the plants re-emerge in the spring.

HOUTTUYNIA CORDATA 'FLORE PLENO'

MINIMUM TEMPERATURE **–25°C (–13°F)**
ZONE **5**

CHARACTERISTICS
Bog garden perennial with roughly heart-shaped, bluish-green foliage flushed with purple. The leaves have an unpleasant odour if bruised. The prominent, fully double, creamy, conelike flowers have an attractive ruff of petals. Height 15–30 cm (6–12 in).

CULTIVATION
Although capable of growing in standing water, it is much better treated as a moisture-loving plant and grown in damp, richly organic soil. Site the plant carefully, since although fully hardy it is very vulnerable to frost damage to the shoots during early spring. Propagate by division once the plants re-emerge in the spring.

HYDROCHARIS MORSUS-RANAE
(Frogbit)

MINIMUM TEMPERATURE **–30°C (–22°F)**
ZONE **4**

CHARACTERISTICS
Hardy, small, floating plant which looks rather like a tiny waterlily. Each plantlet is 5–8 cm (2–3 in) across. The three-petalled white flowers, with a yellow centre, are delicate and papery and appear freely during the summer months. As winter approaches, frogbit produces turions, or winter buds, which fall to the bottom of the pool and reappear during spring when the water warms up.

CULTIVATION
This free-floating plant prospers in a warm, sunny, open position. At the approach of winter, collect the turions and overwinter them in a bowl of water with a little soil in the bottom. Keep the bowl in a frost-free, light environment to encourage early growth the following spring. Propagate by separating and redistributing the plantlets in summer.

IRIS ENSATA
(syn. *I. kaempferi*)
(Japanese clematis-flowered iris/flag)

MINIMUM TEMPERATURE **–20°C (–4°F)**
ZONE **6**

CHARACTERISTICS
One of the most outstanding irises for the bog garden. It produces tufts of broad, grassy or narrow, swordlike foliage with expansive, velvety, deep purple flowers during summer. There are many fine cultivars, including subtle blue 'Queen of the Blues'; soft purplish-pink 'Pink Frost'; rich yellow 'Gold Bound'; and the bold violet-blue flowered 'Variegata', with striking cream and green striped foliage. Height 60–75 cm (24–30 in).

CULTIVATION
All cultivars of *I. ensata* dislike alkalinity, so it is important to mix plenty of peat into the compost. Summer inundation with water is no problem, but during the winter these irises must be kept just moist. Remove faded flower heads. Propagate by division just after flowering.

IRIS LAEVIGATA
(Asiatic water iris)

MINIMUM TEMPERATURE **–20°C (–4°F)**
ZONE **6**

CHARACTERISTICS
An easily grown, hardy, marginal plant, forming clumps of smooth, sword-shaped green leaves. Beautiful blue flowers are produced in midsummer. There are many named cultivars to choose from, including the deep purple-blue and white 'Colchesteri'; soft pink 'Rose Queen'; pure white 'Snowdrift'; and the blue-flowered variegated-leafed 'Variegata'. Height 60–90 cm (2–3 ft).

CULTIVATION
Grow in an open, sunny position in up to 10 cm (4 in) of water in heavy compost. Propagate by dividing established clumps immediately after flowering.

IRIS SIBIRICA
(Siberian iris)

MINIMUM TEMPERATURE **–30°C (–22°F)**
ZONE **4**

CHARACTERISTICS
Excellent, very hardy bog garden plant with vigorous tufts of slender grassy foliage, from which emerge elegant, pale blue flowers, several to a slender stem. There are many cultivars, including the white and creamy yellow 'Butter and Sugar'; dark purple-blue 'Caesar's Brother'; the dwarf, blue-flowered 'Perry's Pygmy'; and rich blue 'Super Ego'. There is also a low-growing, white-flowered kind called 'Little White'. All varieties flower in midsummer. Height 45–90 cm (18–36 in).

CULTIVATION
Grow in an open, sunny position in moist soil. After flowering, remove the faded flower heads. Propagate by dividing established clumps of plants as soon as flowering is over.

IRIS VERSICOLOR
(Blue flag)

MINIMUM TEMPERATURE **–25°C (–13°F)**
ZONE **5**

CHARACTERISTICS
A first-class, marginal plant of compact growth, with plain green swordlike leaves. The flowers are produced in midsummer and are violet-blue and purple, conspicuously marked with creamy yellow. The most widely grown cultivar is the rich plum-coloured 'Kermesina'. Height 45–60 cm (18–24 in).

CULTIVATION
Grow in an open, sunny position in up to 10 cm (4 in) of water in heavy compost. Propagate by dividing established clumps immediately after flowering. The species can also be increased from seed sown in trays of saturated, heavy soil in spring.

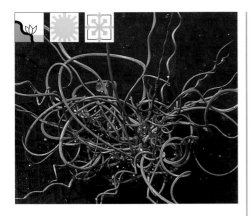

JUNCUS EFFUSUS 'SPIRALIS'
(Corkscrew rush)

MINIMUM TEMPERATURE **–30°C (–22°F)**
ZONE **4**

CHARACTERISTICS
A most curious, hardy marginal plant with dark green, needlelike leaves that are twisted like a corkscrew. During summer it produces small, brownish flowers of little merit; instead, it is grown for its strange, contorted stems. Height 30–45 cm (12–18 in).

CULTIVATION
Grow in any open, sunny position in up to 5 cm (2 in) of water. Any straight stems that are produced should be removed as soon as you see them in order to prevent them from crowding out the desirable contorted growths. Propagate by dividing established plants in spring. Take care to replant only twisted growths.

LAGAROSIPHON MAJOR
(syn. *Elodea crispa*)
(Goldfish weed)

MINIMUM TEMPERATURE **–30°C (–22°F)**
ZONE **4**

CHARACTERISTICS
Totally submerged, hardy aquatic plant with long, dark green succulent stems and dark green, firm foliage. The summer flowers are minute and insignificant. Except in very low temperatures, this is almost always evergreen.

CULTIVATION
Grow completely submerged in a sunny position. In order to maintain health and vigour, replace each spring with short stem cuttings bunched together and attached to a heavy weight. Propagate from cuttings taken during the active growing season.

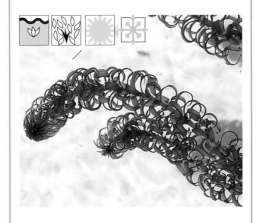

LOBELIA CARDINALIS 'COMPLIMENT SCARLET'

MINIMUM TEMPERATURE **–35°C (–31°F)**
ZONE **3**

CHARACTERISTICS
Moisture-loving perennial for boggy ground, with spires of bright red flowers rising above groups of soft green foliage during late summer. Dies back to overwintering rosettes of foliage in autumn. Height 75–90 cm (30–36 in).

CULTIVATION
Grow in an open, sunny position in wet soil. The plant will tolerate standing in a little water during summer, but will die off in the winter if in anything other than merely damp soil. Although the plant is hardy, some gardeners prefer to lift one or two rosettes of overwintering foliage and place them in slightly drier conditions in a cold frame. Propagate by division in autumn or spring, or from seed sown in a greenhouse very early in the year.

LOBELIA x GERARDII 'VEDRARIENSIS'

MINIMUM TEMPERATURE **–30°C (–22°F)**
ZONE **4**

CHARACTERISTICS

A bold and easily grown moisture-loving
perennial, with intense violet-purple
flowers during late summer. The leaves
are pale green with a strong purple
infusion. Dies back to overwintering
rosettes of foliage in autumn. Height
75–90 cm (30–36 in).

CULTIVATION

Grow in moist soil in a sunny position.
This lobelia will not tolerate standing
water at any time. Propagate by dividing
the overwintering rosettes of foliage
either in autumn or early spring. It is
also easily raised from seed sown during
spring in a cold frame.

LOBELIA x SPECIOSA 'QUEEN VICTORIA'

MINIMUM TEMPERATURE **–30°C (–22°F)**
ZONE **4**

CHARACTERISTICS

Moisture-loving perennial, with
attractive red-purple leaves and spires of
bright scarlet blossoms during late
summer. Dies back to overwintering
rosettes of foliage in autumn. Height
75–90 cm (30–36 in).

CULTIVATION

Grow in an open, sunny position in wet
soil. The plant will tolerate standing in
water for part of the time in summer, but
will die off during the winter if
inundated. Although this species is hardy
to Zone 4, it is a wise precaution to lift
one or two rosettes of overwintering
foliage and place them in slightly drier
conditions in a cold frame. Propagate by
division in autumn or early spring.

LOBELIA SPLENDENS (syn. *L. fulgens*)

MINIMUM TEMPERATURE **–10°C (14°F)**
ZONE **8**

CHARACTERISTICS

Moisture-loving perennial, with purplish-
green or purple leaves and large spires of
scarlet flowers during late summer. A
very variable, but nonetheless beautiful,
plant which dies back in autumn to
overwintering rosettes of foliage. Height
30–60 cm (1–2 ft).

CULTIVATION

Grow in a moist position, preferably in
full sun. This lobelia does not enjoy
standing water at any time. It can survive
quite cold conditions if it remains frozen,
but it is a good idea to lift several
overwintering rosettes of foliage in
autumn and to keep them in a cold frame
as a precaution against winter losses.
Propagate by division in autumn or
spring, or by sowing seed in a greenhouse
during early spring.

LOBELIA SYPHILITICA

MINIMUM TEMPERATURE **–35°C (–31°F)**
ZONE **3**

CHARACTERISTICS
Extremely hardy perennial for wet, boggy conditions. Spires of blue, or very occasionally white, flowers are produced above rather coarse, plain green foliage during summer. The plant dies back during autumn to overwintering rosettes of foliage. Height 30–60 cm (1–2 ft).

CULTIVATION
Grow in full sun or partial shade in moist soil. This lobelia will not tolerate standing in water at any time of the year. Propagate by dividing the overwintering rosettes during spring. Seed can also be sown in spring in a cold frame, but the resulting plants will show variation in flower colour and size.

LYSIMACHIA NUMMULARIA
(Creeping Jenny)

MINIMUM TEMPERATURE **–30°C (–22°F)**
ZONE **4**

CHARACTERISTICS
An easygoing and hardy, more or less evergreen carpeting plant for very wet conditions. It will even grow submerged when given the opportunity. Throughout much of the summer the foliage is studded with bright golden-yellow buttercuplike flowers. The beautiful golden-leafed cultivar 'Aurea' also has yellow flowers. Height 5 cm (2 in).

CULTIVATION
This plant is extremely tolerant of both soil and situation, prospering in sun or shade and in moist soil or standing water. A quite vigorous grower, it benefits from being replaced every second year with fresh cuttings. These root easily in a mixture of equal parts of peat and sharp sand at any time from late spring until late summer.

MATTEUCCIA STRUTHIOPTERIS
(syn. *Struthiopteris germanica*)
(Ostrich fern)

MINIMUM TEMPERATURE **–40°C (–40°F)**
ZONE **2**

CHARACTERISTICS
The most beautiful, hardy, bog garden fern. A large 'shuttlecock' of lacy green foliage is produced around a strong basal crown. Although a very hardy plant, at the first hint of frost the fronds turn a coppery colour and die back. During winter the fern dies back completely to the ground. Height 60–90 cm (2–3 ft).

CULTIVATION
Although a bog plant, this versatile fern is more tolerant than most of inundation and will grow in moist soil or up to 10–15 cm (4–6 in) of water in either full sun or partial shade. Propagate by dividing the creeping rootstock in early spring. Each piece of the creeping rhizome with a green knucklelike shoot is capable of growing into a mature fern.

MENTHA AQUATICA
(Water mint)

MINIMUM TEMPERATURE **–20°C (–4°F)**
ZONE **6**

CHARACTERISTICS
A strongly aromatic, hardy perennial plant with typical mintlike foliage. The dull green leaves are rather downy, and are borne on slender purple or reddish stems. During the summer it produces whorls of soft lilac-pink or pink flowers which are loved by bees. Height 20–45 cm (8–18 in).

CULTIVATION
A vigorously growing plant which prospers in full sun or partial shade in moist soil or as much as 10–15 cm (4–6 in) of water. It is easily propagated from short stem cuttings taken during summer. These should be used regularly to replace older plants that have become woody and untidy.

MIMULUS x HYBRIDUS 'CALYPSO'

MINIMUM TEMPERATURE **–10°C (14°F)**
ZONE **8**

CHARACTERISTICS
Beautiful, exotic-looking, moisture-loving plant with burgundy, red and yellow flowers, which are produced throughout the summer. The petals are flared and the flowers look rather like tropical orchids. The soft green foliage is rounded and forms neat hummocks. The plants die back in the autumn to overwintering rosettes. Height 15–20 cm (6–8 in).

CULTIVATION
Grow in full sun in moist soil, although the plant will tolerate a little standing water during the summer months. Although perennial, it is not long lived and sometimes dies off during the winter. Propagate by dividing overwintered rosettes in spring, or from seed sown in a greenhouse in spring.

MIMULUS x HYBRIDUS 'MALIBU'

MINIMUM TEMPERATURE **–10°C (14°F)**
ZONE **8**

CHARACTERISTICS
Bright orange-flowered hybrid musk with soft green leaves produced in neat mounds. The large, exotic flowers appear throughout much of the summer. The plants die back to overwintering rosettes in autumn. Height 25 cm (10 in).

CULTIVATION
This plant is tolerant of a little standing water during the summer months, but is best grown simply in moist soil. Although perennial, it is not long lived and sometimes dies off during the winter. Propagate from seed sown during the spring in a greenhouse, or by dividing overwintered rosettes in spring.

MIMULUS x HYBRIDUS 'QUEEN'S PRIZE'

MINIMUM TEMPERATURE **–10°C (14°F)**
ZONE **8**

CHARACTERISTICS
A large-flowered, low-growing strain of hybrid musk. It has beautiful, exotic-looking flowers in myriad colours from cream to red, all variously spotted and stained with black, maroon or white. The soft green leaves form low-growing hummocks. The plants die back to overwintering rosettes in autumn. Height 15 cm (6 in).

CULTIVATION
Grow in moist soil, although it will tolerate a little standing water during the summer months. Although perennial, the plant is not long-lived and sometimes dies off during the winter months. Propagate from seed sown in a greenhouse during the spring, or by dividing overwintered rosettes in spring.

MIMULUS LUTEUS
(Yellow musk)

MINIMUM TEMPERATURE **–15°C (5°F)**
ZONE **7**

CHARACTERISTICS
This free-flowering plant is suitable for growing in moist soil or up to 15 cm (6 in) of water. Soft green, rounded foliage is freely produced on a vigorously growing and spreading plant. Spires of bright yellow, tubular flowers give a summer-long display. In autumn the plant dies back to overwintering rosettes of foliage. Height 45–60 cm (18–24 in).

CULTIVATION
Tolerates a little shade, but is much better in full sun in either damp soil or up to 15 cm (6 in) of water. Remove faded flower heads regularly or they will self-seed freely and the plants can become a nuisance. Propagate by dividing the overwintered rosettes of foliage in spring, or by sowing seed at any time during the spring and summer.

MIMULUS RINGENS
(Allegheny monkey flower)

MINIMUM TEMPERATURE **–35°C (–31°F)**
ZONE **3**

CHARACTERISTICS
A branching, slender, marginal plant with handsome, narrow, bright green leaves. The tubular, soft lavender to blue flowers are produced freely on upright spiky stems. During winter the plant dies back completely. Height 40–45 cm (16–18 in).

CULTIVATION
Grow in either damp soil or up to 15 cm (6 in) of water. It prefers full sun, but can tolerate a little shade. Remove faded flower stems to encourage regrowth and, often, a second, less prolific flush of flowers. Easily propagated by division in spring, or from seed sown in a greenhouse during spring or early summer.

MYRIOPHYLLUM AQUATICUM
(syn. M. *proserpinacoides*)
(Parrot feather)

MINIMUM TEMPERATURE **–5°C (23°F)**
ZONE **9**

CHARACTERISTICS
A totally, or sometimes partially, submerged aquatic plant with beautiful feathery foliage. When grown with the foliage above the water, the blue-green, finely cut leaves, produced on scrambling stems, often turn red or orange after the first touch of frost. It is not reliably hardy and is often grown as a greenhouse plant.

CULTIVATION
Although in essence a submerged plant, in a container garden this is best treated as a marginal plant and cultivated in 5–10 cm (2–4 in) of water. If grown outdoors, take a few short stem cuttings during late summer for overwintering. Propagate by removing short stem cuttings, bunching them together with a twist tie, and rooting them in a pot of saturated, heavy soil.

MYRIOPHYLLUM SPICATUM
(Spiked water milfoil)

MINIMUM TEMPERATURE **–20°C (–4°F)**
ZONE **6**

CHARACTERISTICS
Totally submerged aquatic plant with small red and yellowish flower spikes which appear above the surface of the water during summer. The finely divided, filigree foliage is bronze-green and is produced in dense masses on strong, twining, succulent stems. A vigorous plant much liked by fish. Dies back during winter.

CULTIVATION
Grow totally submerged in up to 90 cm (3 ft) of water. A first-class oxygenating plant which requires plenty of light. Propagate from short stem cuttings taken during the spring and summer, fastened together with a twist tie and rooted in saturated, heavy soil.

MYRIOPHYLLUM VERTICILLATUM

MINIMUM TEMPERATURE **–35°C (–31°F)**
ZONE **3**

CHARACTERISTICS
Completely submerged, very hardy aquatic plant with elegant, fine, dark green filigree foliage and very small flowers during the summer. A vigorous plant much utilised by fish fanciers. In winter it dies back almost completely. Very similar to M. *spicatum*, but much more resilient.

CULTIVATION
Grow totally submerged in up to 90 cm (3 ft) of water. An excellent oxygenating plant, it demands an open situation with plenty of light. Propagate from short stem cuttings taken during spring and summer, fastened together with a twist tie, and rooted in saturated, heavy soil. Benefits from regular replacement.

Nymphaea 'Aurora'

Minimum temperature **–20°C (–4°F)**
Zone **6**

Characteristics
Beautiful small-growing waterlily, with attractive purplish and green mottled leaves and handsome flowers which change colour with each passing day. Popularly referred to as a chameleon or changeable waterlily, it starts off with a cream bud which opens to a yellow flower and passes through orange shades to blood red. As the changes take place over several days, a number of different-coloured flowers are in bloom at the same time. Spread 30–60 cm (1–2 ft).

Cultivation
Grow in a heavy aquatic compost in up to 45 cm (18 in) of water. Lift and divide every three or four years. Propagate by division in spring, or by rooting the eyes, which appear with varying frequency on the tuberous rootstock.

Nymphaea caerulea
(Blue lotus)

Minimum temperature **1°C (34°F)**
Zone **10**

Characteristics
This is a tropical waterlily, with starlike, soft blue flowers held above the surface of the water. The round, fresh green, floating foliage is spotted with purple and black. It dies back completely in winter. Spread 45–95 cm (18–38 in).

Cultivation
Grow in up to 60 cm (2 ft) of water in a greenhouse or outdoors in a sunny position, with a consistent temperature of 24°C (75°F). Requires a heavy aquatic compost. Plant in a container and cover the surface with a layer of fine gravel. Store overwintering tubers in trays of damp sand in a frost-free place. Propagate by separating out the tubers during the autumn or by dividing plants in the spring once they have started into growth.

Nymphaea 'Graziella'

Minimum temperature **–20°C (–4°F)**
Zone **6**

Characteristics
The perfect small-growing waterlily for tub culture. Orange-red flowers up to 5 cm (2 in) across, with deep orange stamens, are produced for most of the summer. The olive-green leaves are splashed and spotted with brown and purple. The plant dies back completely in winter. Spread 30–75 cm (12–30 in).

Cultivation
This waterlily requires an open, sunny position. Grow it in a heavy aquatic compost in up to 60 cm (2 ft) of water. Lift and divide the plant every third year. Propagate by division in spring or by rooting the sprouts, or eyes, that appear clustered around the rootstock of the plant.

NYMPHAEA 'LAYDEKERI ALBA'

MINIMUM TEMPERATURE **–20°C (–4°F)**
ZONE **6**

CHARACTERISTICS

An excellent, small-growing waterlily. Its starlike, pure white flowers up to 10 cm (4 in) across have the distinctive aroma of a freshly opened packet of tea. The dark green leaves have a purplish flush beneath. Dies back completely during the winter months. Spread 30–60 cm (1–2 ft).

CULTIVATION

Grow in aquatic compost, ideally in an aquatic planting container, in up to 60 cm (2 ft) of water in an open, sunny position. Every three or four years, lift and divide the plant in spring. Propagate by dividing established plants in spring or by rooting the sprouts, or eyes, that appear at intervals on the woody rootstock.

NYMPHAEA 'LAYDEKERI FULGENS'

MINIMUM TEMPERATURE **–20°C (–4°F)**
ZONE **6**

CHARACTERISTICS

A small-growing waterlily, with starlike, fragrant, bright crimson flowers with reddish stamens. The dark green leaves have purplish undersides and a distinctive brown speckling around the leaf stalk. Dies back completely for the winter months. Spread 30–60 cm (1–2 ft).

CULTIVATION

Grow in aquatic compost, ideally in an aquatic planting container, in up to 60 cm (2 ft) of water in an open, sunny position. Lift and divide the plant in spring every three or four years. Propagate by dividing established plants in spring or by rooting the sprouts, or eyes, that appear at intervals along the woody rootstock.

NYMPHAEA TETRAGONA 'ALBA'
(syn. *N. pygmaea* 'Alba')
(Pygmy white waterlily)

MINIMUM TEMPERATURE **–20°C (–4°F)**
ZONE **6**

CHARACTERISTICS

This is the perfect small waterlily for a sink garden or small tub. Tiny, papery, white flowers scarcely 2.5 cm (1 in) across are produced among small, oval, dark green leaves with purple undersides. The plant dies back completely during the winter. Spread 30–45 cm (12–18 in).

CULTIVATION

Grow in aquatic compost in up to 30 cm (1 ft) of water in an open, sunny position. Lift and replant every two or three years. Propagation is by seed only, since the plant does not produce eyes or divisions. Sow seeds as soon as they ripen in trays of saturated, heavy soil covered by 1 cm (⅜ in) of water in a greenhouse. Prick out the seedlings into individual pots.

NYMPHAEA TETRAGONA 'HELVOLA'
(syn. *N. pygmaea* 'Helvola')

MINIMUM TEMPERATURE **–20°C (–4°F)**
ZONE **6**

CHARACTERISTICS
A very free-flowering, pygmy yellow waterlily. It has beautiful starlike flowers held just above deep olive-green leaves that are liberally splashed and stained with purple and brown. Dies back completely during the winter. Spread 30–45 cm (12–18 in).

CULTIVATION
Grow in soil-based compost in up to 30 cm (1 ft) of water in an open, sunny position. Lift and divide in the spring every third year. Propagate by division in spring, or by rooting the young growths, or eyes, that appear around the base of the rootstock.

NYMPHAEA TETRAGONA 'RUBRA'
(syn. *N. pygmaea* 'Rubra')

MINIMUM TEMPERATURE **–20°C (–4°F)**
ZONE **6**

CHARACTERISTICS
Tiny, blood-red, starlike flowers with orange-red stamens are produced among dark olive-green leaves with a strong purplish cast. The kidney-shaped leaves have distinctive reddish undersides. Dies back completely during the winter. Spread 30–45 cm (12–18 in).

CULTIVATION
Grow in soil-based compost in up to 30 cm (1 ft) of water in an open, sunny position. Since it is not a vigorous grower, this waterlily can be successfully cultivated in a large bucket. Lift and divide in the spring every four or five years. Propagate by occasional division or by the removal and rooting of young growths, or eyes, from the main rootstock, although these are sparingly produced.

ONOCLEA SENSIBILIS
(Sensitive fern)

MINIMUM TEMPERATURE **–30°C (–22°F)**
ZONE **4**

CHARACTERISTICS
A very beautiful, moisture-loving fern which has deeply cut, erect, flattened fronds with a rose pink flush in spring. The fronds eventually turn to a soft lime green hue and by midsummer are mid-green. At the first touch of frost, the fronds wither and die back so that there is nothing to be seen during the winter. Height 45–60 cm (18–24 in).

CULTIVATION
Grow in wet soil or with just a covering of water. Remove faded fronds in the autumn. Propagate by dividing the creeping rootstock in early spring, just as the fronds appear.

PISTIA STRATIOTES
(Water lettuce)

MINIMUM TEMPERATURE **1°C (34°F)**
ZONE **10**

CHARACTERISTICS
This tropical, free-floating plant is, surprisingly, a member of the arum family. It has bold rosettes of soft green, strongly ribbed, downy foliage and produces tiny, green flowers among its leaves. Its general appearance is of a rather fleshy, floating lettuce. Individual plants can grow up to 10 cm (4 in) across and 10 cm (4 in) high, but they usually grow in an interconnected group.

CULTIVATION
Water lettuce generally requires a consistent temperature of about 24°C (75°F) in order to prosper, but it will survive at lower temperatures. It prefers a little shade, although it will grow well in full sun. Take care not to splash the downy foliage with water or else it will suffer from sun scorch. Propagate by dividing and separating the young plants.

PLEIOBLASTUS PYGMAEUS
(syn. *Arundinaria pygmaea*)
(Dwarf bamboo)

MINIMUM TEMPERATURE **–10°C (14°F)**
ZONE **8**

CHARACTERISTICS
Dwarf-growing, finely cut, leafy bamboo with mealy white stems. The mid-green foliage is slightly downy, often with a whitish powdery edge. An evergreen structural plant for a damp position. Height 15–30 cm (6–12 in).

CULTIVATION
Grow in damp soil in an open, sunny position. As stems and foliage fade, remove them from the base. Although hardy to Zone 6, this bamboo is often used for decorative purposes indoors. It grows just as well in the house or greenhouse as in the garden. Propagate by careful division in late spring; use young, outer portions of the plant to grow on, rather than the woody central section.

PONTEDERIA CORDATA
(Pickerel weed)

MINIMUM TEMPERATURE **–35°C (–31°F)**
ZONE **3**

CHARACTERISTICS
A stately, marginal plant, which produces handsome, glossy, green, lance-shaped foliage and strong spikes of soft blue flowers from mid- to late summer. White and pale pink forms are also available. Dies back completely during the winter months. Height 60–90 cm (2–3 ft).

CULTIVATION
Grow in moist soil or in up to 15 cm (6 in) of water in an open, sunny position. Lift and divide the plant in the spring every third year. Propagate by division in spring or by sowing seed, while it is still green, in trays of saturated, heavy soil in late summer. As the seedlings emerge, they should be potted up individually.

POTAMOGETON CRISPUS
(Curled pondweed)

MINIMUM TEMPERATURE **–20°C (–4°F)**
ZONE **6**

CHARACTERISTICS
One of the most beautiful, totally submerged aquatic plants, with bronze-green translucent foliage not unlike that of a seaweed. The leaves are firm and crimped and produced on extensive, scrambling, succulent stems. In midsummer small red flowers are produced just above the surface of the water. The plant dies back to just a few stems during the winter.

CULTIVATION
Grow completely submerged in an open, sunny position. Propagate from short stem cuttings, which are removed during spring or early summer, bunched together with a twist tie, and rooted in pots of saturated, heavy soil. Replace the plants completely at least every second year.

PRIMULA BEESIANA

MINIMUM TEMPERATURE **–20°C (–4°F)**
ZONE **6**

CHARACTERISTICS
Moisture-loving, hardy perennial bog garden plant with bold green, heavily textured foliage. During late spring and early summer it produces strong flower stems with three or more dense whorls of flowers on each. The rosy carmine flowers have a distinctive yellow eye. The plants die back completely during the winter months. Height 60–75 cm (24–30 in).

CULTIVATION
Grow in full sun or partial shade in a damp, richly organic soil. After flowering, remove the old flower heads to prevent self-seeding. Every three or four years lift, divide and replant, ideally as soon as flowering is over. Propagate from seed sown in a cold frame as soon as the seeds ripen. Seed kept for spring sowing will usually need to be frozen for about three weeks in order to break its dormancy.

PRIMULA BULLEYANA

MINIMUM TEMPERATURE **–20°C (–4°F)**
ZONE **6**

CHARACTERISTICS
This moisture-loving, hardy perennial bog garden plant has strong, heavily textured, mid-green foliage. During late spring and early summer it produces tiered whorls of bright orange flowers. The plants die back completely during the winter months. Height 60–75 cm (24–30 in).

CULTIVATION
Grow in full sun or partial shade in damp, richly organic soil. After flowering, remove the old flower heads to prevent self-seeding. Every three or four years lift, divide and replant, ideally as soon as flowering is over. Propagate from seed sown in a cold frame as soon the seed ripen. Seed that is kept for spring sowing will usually require freezing for about three weeks in order to break its dormancy.

PRIMULA DENTICULATA
(Drumstick primula)

MINIMUM TEMPERATURE **–20°C (–4°F)**
ZONE **6**

CHARACTERISTICS
A popular primula that is often grown in the mixed border. Large, globular heads of lilac, pink, purple or white flowers are borne on stout stems. The leaves are green, large and coarse, and have a distinctive aroma; the undersides are often smothered with a white meal that extends up the flower stems. It dies back completely during the winter. Height 30–60 cm (1–2 ft).

CULTIVATION
Grow in full sun or partial shade in damp, richly organic soil. After flowering, remove the old flower heads to prevent self-seeding. Every three or four years lift, divide and replant as soon as flowering is over. Propagate from seed sown in a cold frame as soon as the seeds ripen. Seed kept for spring sowing will usually require freezing for about three weeks in order to break its dormancy.

PRIMULA JAPONICA

MINIMUM TEMPERATURE **–15°C (5°F)**
ZONE **7**

CHARACTERISTICS
A summer-flowering, moisture-loving, hardy perennial, this primula has bold candelabra-shaped heads of deep red flowers on very strong stems. These are produced among clumps of light green, cabbagy leaves. 'Miller's Crimson' is a cultivar with even more intense crimson flowers. Dies back completely during the winter. Height 45–75 cm (18–30 in).

CULTIVATION
Grow in full sun or partial shade in damp, richly organic soil. When flowering is over, remove the old flower heads to prevent self-seeding. Every three or four years lift, divide and replant as soon as flowering is over. Propagate from seed sown in a cold frame as soon as the seeds ripen. Seed that is kept for spring sowing will usually require freezing for about three weeks in order to break its dormancy.

PRIMULA ROSEA

MINIMUM TEMPERATURE **–20°C (–4°F)**
ZONE **6**

CHARACTERISTICS
Low-growing, early spring-flowering perennial bog garden plant with bright rose pink to red flowers, each with a prominent yellow eye. These are produced among soft green leaves, which in early spring have a strong pinkish or purplish flush. Dies back completely for the winter months. Height 15–20 cm (6–8 in).

CULTIVATION
Grow in full sun or with a little shade in a damp, richly organic soil. Every three or four years lift, divide and replant, ideally as soon as flowering is over. Propagate from seed sown in a cold frame as soon as the seeds ripen. Seed that is kept for spring sowing will usually require freezing for about three weeks in order to break its dormancy.

PRIMULA SIKKIMENSIS

MINIMUM TEMPERATURE **–20°C (–4°F)**
ZONE **6**

CHARACTERISTICS
A summer-flowering, moisture-loving, hardy perennial, this primula has bold, green, heavily textured, rounded leaves with a strong, sweet aroma. Elegant heads of pendent funnel-shaped, fragrant, sulphur yellow or creamy yellow flowers are produced on stout stems. Dies back completely during the winter months. Height 45–60 cm (18–24 in).

CULTIVATION
Grow in full sun or partial shade in damp, richly organic soil. When flowering is over, remove the old flower heads to prevent self-seeding. Every three or four years lift, divide and replant as soon as flowering is over. Propagate from seed sown in a cold frame as soon as the seeds ripen. Seed that is kept for spring sowing will usually require freezing for about three weeks in order to break its dormancy.

PRIMULA VIALII
(Orchid primula)

MINIMUM TEMPERATURE **–15°C (5°F)**
ZONE **7**

CHARACTERISTICS
Exotic-looking, hardy perennial bog garden plant with lance-shaped leaves in neat basal tufts. Several short, stout stems protrude from the centre of the plant, each of which ends in a crowded head of small, tubular, red and bluish-purple flowers. This most unusual primula flowers in midsummer. Height 30–45 cm (12–18 in).

CULTIVATION
Grow in full sun or partial shade in a damp, richly organic soil. Remove old flower heads. Unlike most other primulas, this species often dies out naturally after flowering. If clumps persist for a number of years, division and replanting is desirable. Propagate from seed sown in a cold frame as soon as the seeds ripen. Seed that is kept for spring sowing will usually require freezing for about three weeks in order to break its dormancy.

SAGITTARIA LATIFOLIA
(Duck potato)

MINIMUM TEMPERATURE **–15°C (5°F)**
ZONE **7**

CHARACTERISTICS
This hardy, strong-growing, marginal plant produces neat clumps of bold, mid-green, arrow-shaped foliage and spikes of single, three-petalled, white flowers during summer. It dies down completely for the winter months and is often late emerging in the spring. Height 90–120 cm (3–4 ft).

CULTIVATION
Grow in full sun in moist soil or in up to 15 cm (6 in) of water. Protect from waterlily aphids with a systemic insecticide, or knock them off with a strong stream of water from a hose. Lift and separate the overwintered tubers in spring. Propagate by redistributing the tubers.

SAGITTARIA SAGITTIFOLIA 'FLORE PLENO'
(Double arrowhead)

MINIMUM TEMPERATURE **–15°C (5°F)**
ZONE **7**

CHARACTERISTICS
Hardy, marginal plant with clumps of glossy, mid-green, arrow-shaped leaves and strong spikes of papery white, fully double flowers during summer. Dies back completely in the winter and is often late emerging in the spring. Height 30–45 cm (12–18 in).

CULTIVATION
Grow in full sun in moist soil or in up to 15 cm (6 in) of water. Protect from waterlily aphids with a systemic insecticide, or knock them off with a strong stream of water from a hose. Lift and separate the overwintered tubers in spring. Propagate by redistributing the tubers.

SISYRINCHIUM ANGUSTIFOLIUM
(Blue-eyed grass)

MINIMUM TEMPERATURE **–35°C (–31°F)**
ZONE **3**

CHARACTERISTICS
Low-growing, moisture-loving, perennial plant which has very narrow, grasslike leaves produced in tight clumps. In summer, groups of between two and eight starlike or cup-shaped flowers of intense blue with yellow centres are produced on narrow, winged stems among and above the foliage. Height 15–40 cm (6–16 in).

CULTIVATION
Grow in moist soil in an open position. The flowers will only open in full sunlight. Although a perennial plant, it is not always long lived and must sometimes be replaced after a couple of years. While it is possible to divide plants successfully in the spring, the more usual method of Propagation is from seed sown either as soon as the seeds ripen or during early spring, preferably in a cold frame.

SISYRINCHIUM CALIFORNICUM var. BRACHYPUS
(syn. S. brachypus)
(Golden-eyed grass)

MINIMUM TEMPERATURE **–10°C (14°F)**
ZONE **8**

CHARACTERISTICS
Small, moisture-loving, perennial plant with short, swordlike, grey-green leaves growing in tight clumps. Groups of between two and five starlike, bright yellow flowers are produced on narrow, winged stems above the foliage during the summer. Height 15–25 cm (6–10 in).

CULTIVATION
Grow in moist soil in an open position. Full sun is essential if the flowers are to open. Although a perennial plant, it often behaves like an annual. While it is possible in the spring to divide any crowded plants that have overwintered successfully, propagation is usually from seed sown either as soon as the seeds ripen or during early spring, preferably in a cold frame.

STRATIOTES ALOIDES
(Water soldier)

MINIMUM TEMPERATURE **–25°C (–13°F)**
ZONE **5**

CHARACTERISTICS
This hardy, free-floating, perennial aquatic plant looks rather like a narrow-leafed pineapple top. Individual plants can grow up to 20 cm (8 in) across and 15 cm (6 in) deep. It bears creamy white or pinkish papery flowers in the leaf axils. Male flowers appear in clusters, female flowers alone; both are produced during the summer months. During winter the plant sinks to the floor of the pool.

CULTIVATION
Allow to float freely in an open, sunny position. The plant produces young plantlets from runners, which should be detached and redistributed for the purposes of propagation.

TRAPA NATANS
(Water chestnut)

MINIMUM TEMPERATURE **–25°C (–13°F)**
ZONE **5**

CHARACTERISTICS
A handsome, free-floating aquatic plant with rosettes of dark green, rhomboidal leaves and attractive white flowers which grow in the leaf axils. While behaving like a perennial, the water chestnut is really an annual, growing afresh each year from spiny, dark brown nuts which, at the approach of winter, sink to the floor of the pool. They reappear and germinate as the water begins to warm up the following spring.

CULTIVATION
Grow in a sunny position in open water. If left alone, any nuts that have fallen to the pool floor will eventually germinate. If you gather a few nuts in autumn and set them in a frost-free place in a bowl of water with a little soil on the bottom, they will germinate much more quickly and provide early spring foliage.

TYPHA LATIFOLIA
(Greater reedmace)

MINIMUM TEMPERATURE **–35°C (–31°F)**
ZONE **3**

CHARACTERISTICS
Strong-growing, hardy, perennial marginal plant, which has abundant tall, broad, grey-green, swordlike foliage. During late summer and early autumn, from among the leaves arise myriad strong stems, which carry the typical brown, fruiting, pokerlike heads. It is these heads that are often dried and used for indoor floral decorations. Height 90–180 cm (3–6 ft).

CULTIVATION
Grow in an open, sunny position in either moist soil or up to 30 cm (1 ft) of water. This is a very vigorous plant, which needs to be controlled regularly to prevent its fast-growing creeping root system from smothering the roots of its neighbours. Propagate by division in early spring.

TYPHA LAXMANNII

MINIMUM TEMPERATURE **–30°C (–22°F)**
ZONE **4**

CHARACTERISTICS
Strong-growing, hardy, perennial marginal plant, with tall, upright, narrow, grey-green, straplike foliage. Slender, pale brown, pokerlike fruiting heads are produced during late summer and early autumn. These are sometimes dried and used for indoor decoration. Height 90–150 cm (36–60 in).

CULTIVATION
Grow in an open, sunny position in either moist soil or up to 20 cm (8 in) of water. A vigorous plant, it should be carefully controlled to ensure that it does not smother any weaker-growing neighbours. Propagate by division during early spring.

TYPHA MINIMA
(Dwarf reedmace)

MINIMUM TEMPERATURE **–20°C (–4°F)**
ZONE **6**

CHARACTERISTICS
An easygoing, marginal plant for the smaller water feature, especially a tub or sink garden. It is a complete miniature replica of the common reedmace, with dark green, grassy foliage and short, chunky, rounded, dark brown seed heads. Unlike its relatives, this species is not invasive. Height 45 cm (18 in).

CULTIVATION
Grow in an open, sunny position in moist soil or in up to 5 cm (2 in) of water. Every three or four years, it will need dividing during early spring. Propagate by division in early spring.

VALLISNERIA SPIRALIS
(Tape grass, Eelgrass)

MINIMUM TEMPERATURE **1°C (34°F)**
ZONE **10**

CHARACTERISTICS
Tropical, submerged aquatic plant forming neat clumps of narrow, tapelike, translucent green leaves. Once established, it creeps around, eventually developing into sizeable colonies. The flowers are minute. Tape grass remains green unless the water temperature drops below 5°C (41°F).

CULTIVATION
Grow in a sandy soil in up to 30 cm (1 ft) of water in full sun or partial shade. Replace the plants regularly every two years in order to maintain vigour. Propagate by dividing clumps of plantlets at any time during the growing season.

VERONICA BECCABUNGA
(Brooklime)

MINIMUM TEMPERATURE **−25°C (−13°F)**
ZONE **5**

CHARACTERISTICS
Hardy, semi-evergreen, marginal plant with scrambling stems clothed in dark green, rounded foliage. Dark blue flowers, each with a conspicuous white eye, cover the plant throughout the summer. During most winters, the plant remains green, but if the temperature drops below −20°C (−4°F) it is likely to lose its leaves. Height 15–20 cm (6–8 in).

CULTIVATION
Grow in moist soil or in up to 15 cm (6 in) of water. It is an ideal plant for disguising the edge of a water feature. Although it is a perennial, much better plants result from regular replacement by short stem cuttings taken during early spring. Propagate from stem cuttings taken at any time during the growing season, or by lifting and detaching shoots that have rooted in saturated, heavy soil or water.

ZANTEDESCHIA AETHIOPICA
(White arum lily)

MINIMUM TEMPERATURE **0°C (32°F)**
ZONE **10**

CHARACTERISTICS
A striking, perennial marginal plant with handsome, heart-shaped, bright green leaves and white, funnel-like petals (spathes), each with a slender, yellow central flower spike (spadix). Dies back during the winter. There are a number of cultivars, among them the slightly smaller and hardier 'Crowborough', and 'Green Goddess', with pale green flowers. Height 60–120 cm (2–4 ft).

CULTIVATION
Grow in up to 30 cm (1 ft) of water in a greenhouse or outdoors in a warm climate or over the summer. When growing in deep water, frost is usually tolerated. If waterlily aphids attack the plant, use a systemic insecticide or knock them off with a strong stream of water from a hose. Lift and divide every third year, just as the plants start into growth. Propagate by dividing and redistributing the tubers.

ZANTEDESCHIA ELLIOTTIANA
(Yellow arum lily)

MINIMUM TEMPERATURE **1°C (34°F)**
ZONE **10**

CHARACTERISTICS
Wonderful tropical, perennial, marginal plant with bold, heart-shaped, dark green leaves that are heavily spotted with white. Beautiful bright yellow, funnel-like petals (spathes) are produced during the summer. Dies back during the winter unless high light intensity and warmth can be maintained. Height 60–80 cm (24–32 in).

CULTIVATION
Grow in up to 20 cm (8 in) of water indoors in tropical conditions, ideally with a consistent temperature of 24°C (75°F). Protect from waterlily aphids with a systemic insecticide, or knock them off with a strong stream of water from a hose. Lift and divide every third year, just as the plants start into growth. Propagate by dividing and redistributing the tubers.

Hardiness Zones

❧

The temperatures given in these maps indicate the lowest temperature or range of temperatures a plant will tolerate.

Each plant in the Directory
has a number that corresponds with the zone maps illustrated here. Once you know what climatic zone you live in, you can tell at a glance whether or not a particular plant will thrive in your garden, or if it needs winter protection.

Remember that hardiness is not just a question of minimum temperatures. A plant's ability to survive certain temperatures is affected by many factors, such as the amount of shelter given and its position within your garden.

KEY
Average annual minimum temperature

Zone 1		*Below -45°C (-50°F)*
Zone 2		*-45 to -40°C (-50 to -40°F)*
Zone 3		*-40 to -34°C (-40 to -30°F)*
Zone 4		*-34 to -29°C (-30 to -20°F)*
Zone 5		*-29 to -23°C (-20 to -10°F)*
Zone 6		*-23 to -17°C (-10 to 0°F)*
Zone 7		*-17 to -12°C (0 to 10°F)*
Zone 8		*-12 to -7°C (10 to 20°F)*
Zone 9		*-7 to -1°C (20 to 30°F)*
Zone 10		*-1 to 5°C (30 to 40°F)*

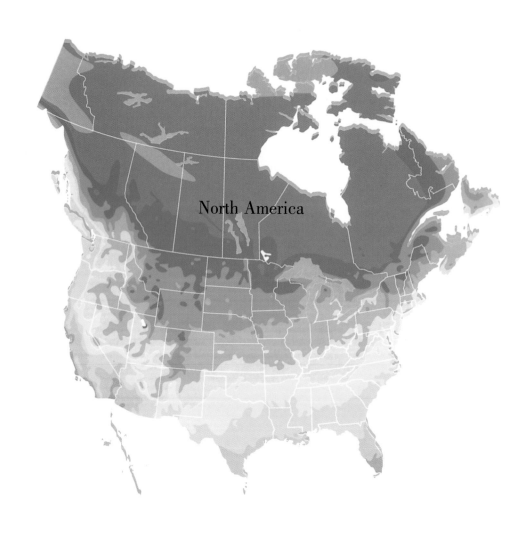

North America

Zone 1		Below -45°C (-50°F)
Zone 2		-45 to -40°C (-50 to -40°F)
Zone 3		-40 to -34°C (-40 to -30°F)
Zone 4		-34 to -29°C (-30 to -20°F)
Zone 5		-29 to -23°C (-20 to -10°F)
Zone 6		-23 to -17°C (-10 to 0°F)
Zone 7		-17 to -12°C (0 to 10°F)
Zone 8		-12 to -7°C (10 to 20°F)
Zone 9		-7 to -1°C (20 to 30°F)
Zone 10		-1 to 5°C (30 to 40°F)

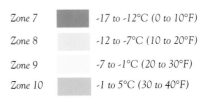

Zone 7		-17 to -12°C (0 to 10°F)
Zone 8		-12 to -7°C (10 to 20°F)
Zone 9		-7 to -1°C (20 to 30°F)
Zone 10		-1 to 5°C (30 to 40°F)

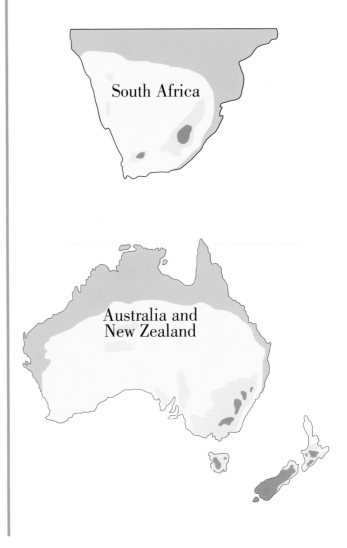

Europe

South Africa

Australia and
New Zealand

Things You Need to Know

❧

General Considerations

Position is everything with a water feature. It is essential that you choose an open, sunny spot and preferably one that is sheltered. Full, uninterrupted sunlight is crucial for the successful growth of most aquatic plants. It is particularly important in ensuring that plants such as irises and waterlilies, which are grown for their flowers, bloom well and for the longest possible period. You should keep your water feature well away from trees, since they shed troublesome leaves.

Shelter is necessary in order to protect plants from damaging cold winds in early spring, and also to reduce evaporation. When moving water is to be a highlight, you should utilise a quiet corner, as strong breezes blow the water about and might spoil the effect. Indoors, ventilation during summer months and some shade, if the pool is in a conservatory, are essential.

If you are planning to use moving water, make sure that sources of electricity and fresh water are close by to operate the pump. If you

MOVING WATER
A fountain adds character to a small container.

need to install an electricity supply, always have the work done by a qualified electrician.

Stability is important, especially for taller containers and where there are young children around, since water is heavy and can easily overbalance a top-heavy urnlike feature that is not secured to the ground. There are

many strong adhesives that are very effective, but remember that if your container is not frostproof you may need to bring it indoors for the winter, and any ground fixing should take this into account.

Small water features have much in common with garden pools, but they can

never attain the natural balance that is achieved in a pool. With a traditional garden pool, plants and animals interact harmoniously to create a miniature underwater world. In a container or small water feature, this is not possible. The main reason for this is the wide range of temperatures that such a feature experiences. Sudden soaring temperatures, combined with a high level of nutrients, can create a green algal bloom in a matter of hours. Such intense warmth can also lead to oxygen depletion and the rapid demise of any fish. So, in many containers fish cannot be used.

Routine maintenance is, however, much like that for any garden pond, including regular deadheading of plants, removal of algae and checking for troublesome aphids.

Make sure to select an appropriate growing medium for the plants in your container water garden – garden soil will not do. The planting mixture must be able to sustain healthy growth, but at the same time it must not leach nutrients

into the water or cause pollution. Use a soil-based medium, preferably one that has been specially formulated for aquatic plants. The compost should ideally be heavy, and any organic matter must be well decayed.

The choice of appropriate plants is important, as many aquatic subjects are fast growing and can become ungainly. Select plants of a naturally modest stature so that any cutting back necessary to keep them within bounds is scarcely noticeable. In many instances, the plants need to be of an easygoing disposition and you must be able to transplant them successfully.

TAKING CARE
Although easy to maintain, a container water feature needs regular attention.

GETTING THE POSITION RIGHT
Make sure that your container is in an open, sunny position, but also close to a convenient supply of fresh water and electricity.

① *Submersible pump*
② *Plastic tubing that supplies water to the upper container from the pump outlet*
③ *End of tubing, fed through ornamental pump*
④ *Buried electricity point feeding pump and optional light*
⑤ *Vertical windbreak*

Pumps and Fountains

Moving water plays an important role in many container water features. Indeed, the reason for having such a small feature is often that it offers an opportunity to have safe, moving water in the garden or on the patio.

All you need to produce moving water are a suitable pump and a simple understanding of both flow rates and filtration. You can greatly enhance the clarity of the water by using a filter attached to the pump; in many instances a simple filter unit will already be built into the pump.

Almost all small water features can be served by a submersible pump. These come in a wide range of shapes and sizes and usually sit in the container underneath the water and recirculate it as a fountain or waterfall. Some pumps require the installation of a separate, buried cable. But there are many low-voltage pumps, and the cable for these can be run on the surface and disguised by plants. It must, however, be protected by plastic conduit where people are going to walk over it. For most small water features, low-voltage pumps are perfectly adequate. Only if significant

CASCADING FOUNTAIN
The water is the feature here, as conditions are not suitable for plants.

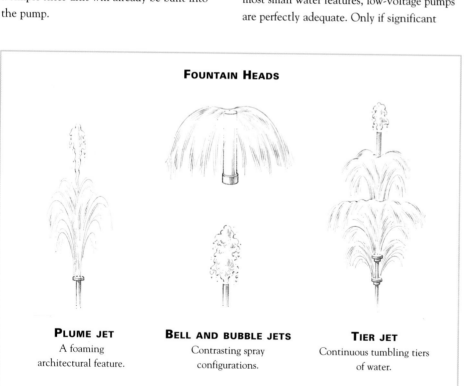

FOUNTAIN HEADS

PLUME JET
A foaming architectural feature.

BELL AND BUBBLE JETS
Contrasting spray configurations.

TIER JET
Continuous tumbling tiers of water.

BELL FOUNTAIN FEATURE
Plants can live happily with gently moving water.

Things You Need to Know **118**

amounts of water are to be moved will you need a more powerful unit. The provision of the power-supply cable and the method of hiding it are the biggest challenges anyone creating a moving water feature has to contend with.

If you would like to construct a straightforward fountain in a sizeable, uncluttered container, there is another option. Recently, a small solar-powered fountain has been developed that works without electricity. It consists of a small, round unit with a built-in pump and a solar panel that is placed on the surface of the water. The height of the fountain jet varies according to the weather, but on a warm, sunny day a jet 30–50 cm (12–20 in) high can be expected.

Whatever configuration of moving water you decide on, it is important to get the flow rate of the water right. When choosing a pump, always select one that will deliver slightly more water over a given time than is required. Having spare capacity allows you to change the type of fountain if you wish to, and since the pump does not need to work at full capacity all the time there is no strain on it and its life is extended.

Volume requirements and movements for most small contained features are modest, and calculations based on standard practice may need to be adapted and scaled down. Broadly speaking, in order to assess a pump's capacity for a flowing feature, pour water over a cascade unit or something similar from a

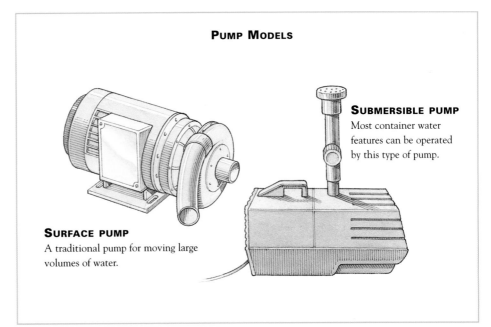

PUMP MODELS

SUBMERSIBLE PUMP
Most container water features can be operated by this type of pump.

SURFACE PUMP
A traditional pump for moving large volumes of water.

garden hose at the rate desired. Collect the water delivered over the period of one minute. Measure the quantity that is collected in litres (quarts), multiply by 60, and you have the number of litres (quarts) per hour that the pump must be able to move to produce the desired result. Potential fountain heights are generally described on the packaging of a pump.

The type of fountain spray created depends on which jet you choose. Jets are detachable and merely push or screw on to the pump outlet. There are many different patterns of spray, and also attachments that will ensure a constantly changing sequence – in the most sophisticated cases this can be synchronised with lights and music.

MOVING WATER AND PLANTS
This delightful arrangement combines moving water with the happy establishment of plants.

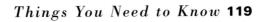

Keeping Water Clear

Small water features are always more difficult to keep clear than large ponds. With a small volume of water, rapid temperature change leads to the growth of algae and oxygen depletion, and in winter it is difficult to sustain a balance of life. Water quality depends on a balanced environment, which is impossible to achieve in anything less than a modest garden pool.

Discolouration of the water, other than from algae, is usually a physical indication that something has gone badly wrong. Perhaps there is a dead and rotting fish or plant, or growing medium has spilled or leached into the water.

In all small water features green water will appear from time to time. The first thing to do to reduce its occurrence is to select your medium very carefully. A compost that is high in readily soluble nutrients will create nightmare green conditions, so avoid using ordinary garden compost at all cost. Properly formulated aquatic compost contains a minimum of soluble fertiliser and plants depend upon regular feeding with a tablet form of slow-release fertiliser that is manufactured for the precise requirements of aquatic plants. If submerged and floating

WEEDS
Silkweed or flannel weed can completely obscure the water surface.

REMOVING ALGAE
Filamentous algae can only be controlled by hand.

plants are the only aquatics grown, you can use washed fine gravel and the container can remain soilless. If one or two fish can be included they will provide sufficient detritus, along with the natural plant detritus, for the nourishment of the plants.

Although it is true that a permanent natural balance cannot be achieved in a small water feature, submerged plants can make some difference. As well as being oxygenators, they mop up excess nutrients which are then not available for algal growth, and this helps to keep the water clear.

Without a natural balance, the only reliable way to keep the water clear is by the use of algicides. These are particularly effective with suspended algae – some simply kill them, others cause the algae and other organic detritus to form a mat and settle on the floor of the container. The range of algicides available is huge and, provided that they are used exactly as prescribed on the packaging, neither plants, fish, nor snails will suffer.

Filamentous algae presents a different problem. This is variously known as silkweed, blanket weed or flannel weed, and it can only be successfully removed by hand. An algicide will kill it, but you still need to remove it in order to prevent it from deoxygenating the water when decomposing. The regular removal of filamentous algae should therefore be part of routine maintenance.

Dirty water resulting from other causes usually means that the feature has to be emptied and cleaned. This is very simple if the death of a fish or plant has caused the

pollution, but it can be a little more troublesome to prevent soil or compost spillage recurring.

When planted areas are clearly defined, topdressing the compost with a shallow layer of fine gravel will prevent soil from escaping into the water and deter fish from stirring up the soil. When this is not practical, use a piece of old tights, fill it with soil and mould it to the shape of the planting pocket; the fabric retains all but the finest particles of soil. You can insert the plants through holes

that are just large enough to accommodate them, and the roots will bind the whole package together, preventing spillage.

ALGAE CONTROL

Make sure that your container has fresh and clean water at all times.

Fish and Snails

Fish can be an important component of any water feature, although in some of the smaller types they would not be able to survive a cold winter, or even a very warm summer. A substantial volume of cool water can help to sustain animal life but, for the most part, it is the amount of water surface area available that is crucial to the survival of fish. The larger the surface area, the more oxygen is available. In many containers, irrespective of the surface area available, the violent temperature changes that often occur in a small volume of water make it impractical to introduce fish.

While not essential, fish add considerable visual interest to a small water garden. They cannot do much to bring about a natural balance, but they are extremely useful in controlling aquatic insect pests, especially mosquito larvae. Where it is not possible to keep fish, a small amount of cooking oil dropped on to the water every few weeks prevents the larvae from coming up for air and is harmless to plants. Alternatively you can use mosquito dunks, an import from the United States, to eliminate these pests. These release an innocuous chemical into the water that is nevertheless deadly to the active larvae.

If you are able to include fish in your feature, always select small specimens. Fish are remarkable creatures which are able to adapt to their environment by restricting their growth to the space available. Thus a

CHOOSING FISH
These fish are suitable for container water gardens.

Shubunkin

Comet

Bubble Eye

WHAT TO LOOK FOR WHEN BUYING FISH

EYES
These should be bright and clear.

FINS
These should be erect and entire.

BODY
This should have no scales missing.

GOOD HEALTH
There should be no trail of faeces.

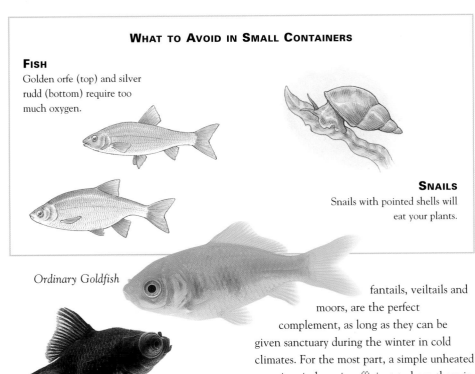

Ordinary Goldfish

Moor

small goldfish kept in a goldfish bowl for four or five years will be much the same size as when it was first introduced, and will be quite healthy and lively. Once placed in a garden pond, the same goldfish will grow rapidly and can double its size within six months. So it is essential, if your fish are to live a healthy life, that you use small specimens from the outset.

Not all fish, even small ones, will enjoy or tolerate the constraints of a container water feature. Those with high oxygen requirements, such as golden orfe and silver rudd, will quickly perish. Fancy goldfish, especially fantails, veiltails and moors, are the perfect complement, as long as they can be given sanctuary during the winter in cold climates. For the most part, a simple unheated aquarium indoors is sufficient to keep them in good condition all through the winter.

When selecting fish it is important to choose those that have bright eyes and erect fins, and appear lively and active (although this may be the result of keeping the fish hungry so that they dart about attractively and do not create too much pollution in the dealer's tank). A clean body without any kind of fungal disease and with all the scales intact is vital; and there should be no sign of constipation from trailing faeces.

Snails can also be introduced to a water feature to some advantage. If you use the ramshorn type, they will keep much of the troublesome filamentous algae under control, especially algae clinging to the inside of the container. Ramshorn snails are round, flat and disclike, and carry their shells upright on their backs. In very warm conditions they often succumb to the heat, and in heavily populated containers they are sometimes sucked out of their shells by the fish and devoured. Avoid pointed snails or freshwater whelks, which are often sold for water gardens. While it is true that they will eat algae, they will much prefer your prize waterlily.

Fish and snails tend to look after themselves quite well if they have sufficient room and protective plant cover. In a balanced environment there is enough food available naturally for the fish to survive, but in a confined space feeding the fish is essential and fun. Give a good-quality food sparingly three times a week during the summer, never more than the fish can clear up in 20 minutes.

RAMSHORN SNAIL
This snail grazes on algae rather than plants.

Calender of Care

Small water features can require almost as much attention as a large garden pond. The time taken to carry out tasks may be much less, but it is necessary to be just as vigilant in ensuring that all is well.

The advice given for autumn and winter applies mainly to colder climates.

Spring

This is the best time to create a container water feature and to plant it and install moving water if you wish to.

Carry out new plantings in existing features and introduce fish where appropriate.

Reintroduce overwintered plants and, where appropriate, divide them. Lift and divide crowded clumps of plants that have remained in the open.

Fertilise established plants, using specially formulated aquatic plant fertiliser tablets or sachets pushed into the soil next to the plants.

Feed fish if the weather is warm and they are swimming around actively.

Summer

There is still time to plant and establish a new water feature. Later plantings do not flower as freely as those made during the spring, but they are still worthwhile. Fish can be introduced at any time during the summer months.

Keep a close watch for green and discoloured water and use an algicide if necessary. You can treat blanketweed and other filamentous algae chemically, but they must still be removed by hand to prevent them from decomposing and deoxygenating the water.

As flowering plants fade, remove the old heads and flower stalks. It is not only tidier to do this, but the plants' energy is conserved by preventing them from setting seed. Also remove dead leaves regularly.

DEADHEADING
It is important to remove dead heads regularly.

Keep an eye open for any pests and diseases that may affect the plants. Troublesome aphids are easily disposed of with a strong jet of water or by using a systemic insecticide.

USING FERTILISER SACHETS

To prevent nutrients escaping into the water and creating a green algal bloom, use sachets of aquatic plant fertiliser. Tear off the protective strip to reveal the perforations and place in the compost next to each plant. Top dress with fine gravel.

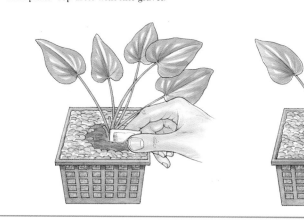

Autumn

With the approach of autumn, tidy up all the plants and remove those that are going to be overwintered indoors from their containers. To overwinter most aquatic plants successfully, plant them close together in deep trays of damp compost in a frost-free place. In warmer climates, where the temperature does not drop below –5°C (23°F), many hardy aquatics are best left where they are to overwinter.

The turions, or overwintering buds, of floating plants such as *Hydrocharis morsus-ranae* (frogbit), and the spiky nuts of *Trapa natans* (water chestnut) usually overwinter on the floor of the pool. If you intend to empty the container for the winter, gather a few turions and place them in a bucket of water with a little soil on the bottom; they will keep successfully until spring. Such tactics are essential if the plants are to be preserved. Even when they would normally be allowed to remain where they are, it is advantageous to be able to start them indoors, particularly if the spring season is late getting under way.

Treat any lingering algae with an algicide and, where appropriate, empty the containers and bring them inside in preparation for the winter.

Winter

For the small container water garden, winter is not the best time. While it is feasible to retain one or two features, such as a sunken barrel or a lion mask, in good order outside, in general containers are best drained, cleaned and placed in a frost-free place for the winter.

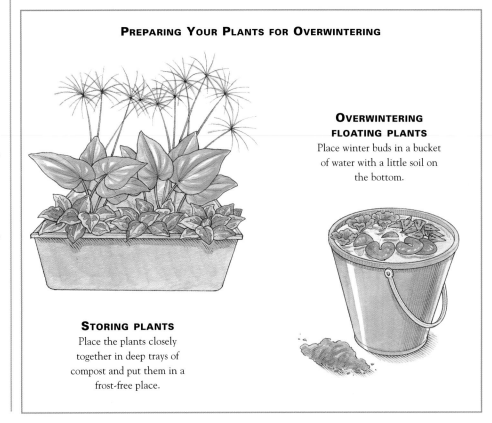

PREPARING YOUR PLANTS FOR OVERWINTERING

OVERWINTERING FLOATING PLANTS
Place winter buds in a bucket of water with a little soil on the bottom.

STORING PLANTS
Place the plants closely together in deep trays of compost and put them in a frost-free place.

Index

Credits

Quarto would like to acknowledge and thank the following for
providing pictures reproduced in this book: **The Garden Picture
Library**: 6 (John Glover), 7 (Lamontagne), 8 (Ron Sutherland), 9t
(John Glover), 10l & r (John Glover), 11l (David Askham), 12
(Steven Wooster), 13 (Mayer/Le Scanff), 109 (Brian Carter), 110tl
(Didier Willery); **Jerry Pavia:** 11r, 92c, 93c & r; **Harry Smith
Collection:** 3, 88c, 102c, 111c, 116, 117, 118t & b, 119, 120t & b, 121.
Key: r=right, l=left, t=top, b=bottom, c=centre

Quarto would also like to thank the following for permission to take
location photographs: Anglo-Aquarium Plant Company Ltd, London,
UK; London Aquatic Ltd, London, UK; Royal Botanical Gardens, Kew,
UK. We would also like to thank the project maker, Ian Howes; and
Sally Roth (US) and Frances Hutchison (Australia) for checking the
plant directory.

The author would like to thank the following for providing plants and
equipment: Jackie Barber, Littlethorpe Nurseries, Ripon, UK; Tropica
Aquarium and Water Garden Centre, Moorland Nurseries,
Knaresborough, UK; Thirsk Tropical Fish and Water Garden Centre,
Thirsk, UK; Oland Plants, Sawley, Ripon, UK.

The index was prepared by Dorothy Frame.

Product code 40-985